Chaplain Thom...,

Praying Numbers 6:24-26 over you & your family! Lift Your Gaze!

Deep Waters:
Lift Your Gaze

Kim M. Clark

Deep Waters: Lift Your Gaze.

Published by Deep Waters Books, P.O. Box 692301, Orlando, FL 32869, www.deepwatersbooks.com

Cover Design: Pamela Lentz
Cover Art: a&b photo/video, photodune, envatomarket

First Printing 2018
Printed in the United States of America

All emphases in Scripture quotations have been added by the author.

Identifiers: ISBN 978-1-7327480-1-9 (Hardcover) | 978-0-692-12003-3 (pbk.) | 978-1-7327480-0-2 (epub) | LCCN 2018907696

Publisher's Cataloging-in-Publication data
Names: Clark, Kim M., author.
Title: Deep waters : lift your gaze / Kim M. Clark.
Description: Orlando, FL : Deep Waters Books, 2018.
Identifiers: ISBN 978-1-7327480-1-9 (Hardcover) | 978-0-692-12003-3 (pbk.) | 978-1-7327480-0-2 (epub) | LCCN 2018907696
Subjects: LCSH Christian life. | Bible--Study and teaching. | Faith. | Christian women--Religious life. | Suffering--Religious aspects--Christianity. | Bereavement--Religious aspects—Christianity. | Grief--Religious aspects--Christianity. | Consolation. | BISAC RELIGION / Christian Life / Personal Growth | RELIGION / Christian Life / Death, Grief, Bereavement | RELIGION / Christian Life / Women's Issues
Classification: LCC BV4527 .C544 2018 | DDC 248.8/43--dc23

Dedication

I lovingly dedicate this book to J.B. and J.C.
May you both always lift your gaze
to your God.

Contents

Trial: *noun* | tri-al

a test of faith, patience or

stamina through subjection

to suffering or temptation[1]

Foreword

THERE ARE SEVERAL subjects that Christians are not in agreement about and hold diverse views and interpretation on. One of those subjects is trials and suffering. How often do we hear someone ask, "Why do Christians suffer?" or "Why does God allow bad things to happen to good people?" These and related questions cannot not be ignored or brushed off as irrelevant. God's people face them daily.

While some Christian scholars, authors, and theologians have avoided tackling the important subject of trials and suffering, Kim M. Clark has done a commendable job of taking the bull by its horns in authoring *Deep Waters: Lift Your Gaze*. She has faithfully, practically, and biblically addressed the inevitability of trials, the reason for trials, our response to trials, and our greatest need.

The inclusion, in each chapter, of a topical biblical story and perspective on seeking God during today's trials is uplifting and edifying, and the accompanying prophetic words and poems are precious and superb. It is the very depths of the poignant application questions and prayer journal at the end of each chapter that inspire the reader to lift their gaze to God and away from their trials, troubles, frustrations, challenges, and temptations.

Kim is not some ivory-tower author. Her concern and care for her readers is demonstrated in the last section of each chapter, where she pours out her heartfelt intercessory prayer for each reader. As a scholar, author, and Christian educator, I found this aspect of each chapter to be unique, spiritual, and inspiring.

I would highly recommend *Deep Waters: Lift Your Gaze* to any reader who hungers to study, understand, and appreciate the what and why of trials and suffering. Kim's faith, zeal, and passion will no doubt encourage readers to not focus their gaze on trials and suffering but to fix their eyes "on Jesus, the pioneer and perfecter of faith. For the joy set before him he endured the cross, scorning its shame, and sat down at the right hand of the throne of God. Consider him who endured such opposition from sinners, so that you will not grow weary and lose heart" (Hebrews 12:2–3 NIV).

Dr. Wilbroad Chanda
Pastor, Christ Community Church
Principal, Copperbelt Pastors College
Zambia, Africa

SECTION I

The Nature of Trials

FORETASTE

Deep Waters

"Fear not, for I have redeemed you; I have called you by name, you are mine. When you pass through the waters, I will be with you; and through the rivers, they shall not overwhelm you; when you walk through fire you shall not be burned, and the flame shall not consume you. *For I am the Lord your God, the Holy One of Israel, your Savior."*

~ Isaiah 43:1–3 *emphasis mine*

I was beyond overwhelmed—felt like I was drowning in deep waters. A struggling single mom of a small child, I was working for a Christian mission organization and things were beyond tight financially. Taking this job had been a step in faith; the salary was only an eighth of what I'd made as an information technology sales and marketing executive. Now my savings were depleted, the bills were stacking up, and I had no idea how to make ends meet.

As I ran my hands through my hair, I crumbled into a sobbing mess on my desk. The budget numbers didn't add up. My expenses exceeded my income exponentially. I had cut everything I possibly could and had even stopped eating meals to save money. It was futile. Nothing was working.

I didn't have the strength to go on anymore. Sleep evaded me. I was weary—hungry, tired, and lonely. Doing everything on my own was too hard. I was responsible for all the home care and child-rearing, acting as decision maker, plumber, disciplinarian, homework helper, cook, maid, income earner, nurse, counselor, chauffeur, gardener, cupcake baker, fireman, gutter cleaner, booboo kisser, repairman, and anything-else-that-needed-to-be-done person.

I was *it*, and *it* was exhausted.

Shaking my fist, I cried out to God, "You brought me here! I told you I wanted to work for your kingdom. I trusted that you would take care of things. Your word says, 'Seek the kingdom of God and his righteousness and all these things will be provided for you'" (Matt 6:33 HCSB).

After a deep breath, my angry monologue continued, "And I've sought you with my whole heart, but I'm missing the providing part, God! I need your help!"

Shoulders slumped, I whimpered. Then I paced back and forth across my office. Finally, I flopped back down in my office chair completely dejected.

I didn't think about how God had always provided for me, how he always came through, or how even as a single mom I was able to afford to send my child to an expensive private school, drive a clean, dependable Honda sedan with leather seats and a sunroof, and live in a three-bedroom, two-and-half-bath home with a tall wooden fenced-in backyard in a safe neighborhood—all on a ministry salary. Nope, I was focused solely on what I perceived was my all-encompassing life problem: not enough money (that I could see) in the bank to pay the bills.

I was looking at my life through the eyes of the flesh, not the eyes of faith.

Taking another deep breath and slowly exhaling, I reminded myself of the definition of faith: "to be sure of the things we hope for, certain of what we cannot see" (Hebrews 11:1 GNT).

> Definition of faith: "to be sure of the things we hope for, certain of what we cannot see"
>
> ~ Hebrews 11:1

At the end of my own strength and sufficiency, I prayed. I laid my hands on my bills and declared, "God, these are yours. I did what you asked. I took a job to work for your kingdom. Please provide the funds each month to meet all my bills. In Jesus' name I pray."

Interestingly enough, things didn't turn around quickly. I still had that sickening feeling every time a letter with a due date came in the mail. I would try not to cry. Looking up, I would say, "I trust you despite what it looks like, God."

Drawing on my creativity, I found fun things to do that didn't cost money. My little one and I went to the park, the library, and every free festival in town. I strived to keep on a happy face, be a good mommy, and laugh often—even though we were sinking deeper into financial abyss.

Maybe you too are experiencing a fire so intense that you might think God has forgotten you. Even the thought of taking another step is paralyzing. Perhaps you've also prayed for this difficult situation to be taken from you, but it remains like a weight crushing your chest, making living near impossible. Or maybe you know someone who is going through a horrific trial and your heart breaks for them.

Even though we all know hardships are a part of life, no matter how much we pray, they are still brutal. Trials hurt. No one is exempt from the pain. Beyond a shadow of a doubt, we will and do suffer while on earth. Just browse any newsfeed to witness the horrors.

One thing I've realized is that the pain from our trials provides a unique opportunity for exponential growth. It is during those dark times that we mine deep into resources we never knew we had. We uncover that burst of strength and peace that we didn't know even existed. Then, and only then, are we able to pull out of our pain and suffering.

Thankfully, when we are weak, God is strong. He even declares it: "'My grace is sufficient for you, for my power is made perfect in weakness.' … For when I am weak, then I am strong" (2 Corinthians 12:9–10). He is faithful. He knows our prayers and the desires of our heart before we even formulate them (Romans 8:37).

Even with faith in God, receiving comfort can be difficult. When I was walking through our trial, instead of getting better, my heart seemed to break even more. Reading the Bible, receiving wise counsel, and praying only provided temporary solace. Sometimes I experienced waves of tranquility, but how quickly could one errant thought or word suck me back into the powerful rip currents of despair. It was a constant battle for me. Actually doing menial tasks was heart-wrenching as one morning I wept while making breakfast for my four-year-old. Beautiful brown eyes looked at me with compassion as my preschooler wisely declared, "Don't cry Mommy. You have Jesus."

I smiled, wiped my eyes, and silently whispered, "Out of the mouth of babes." Then I got down on my knees and dissolved into an emotional puddle. I prayed for enough strength to get through the day as little, warm, sticky arms wrapped around my neck and squeezed me tight.

> "Don't cry, Mommy. You have Jesus."
>
> ~ My preschooler

Trusting God in our darkest moments requires a degree of fortitude that isn't natural. This forced act of obedience is available only through the grace of God. I remember both physically and spiritually struggling to lift my gaze to him. It is during these dark times that I have been blessed to hear God speak to my heart through his Holy Spirit. And it is through those words that I have received great comfort and peace.

One day as I walked along a sandy shoreline with my child playing nearby, I angrily forced my toes into the wet sand and brooded over my situation. I was oblivious to the joy of the beach, the laughter of children, and the comfort coming from crashing waves. It was then I heard the Lord speak to my heart...

Deep Waters

O afflicted one, storm-tossed and not comforted, I see your pain. Lift your gaze. Look at me. Focus on me, not your problems or concerns. You are mine. I have you. And I have this.

Do you trust me? Do you see the waters?

Look to the left, look straight out, and look to the right.

Do you see an end to my waters?

I carry them all in the palm of my hand. For I have measured them. They are mine. As is everything teeming in them.

I know your heart. I know it is heavy. For I know your pain. I formed the earth and laid its foundations. I knew you before you were even conceived. I knew you would be facing this trial. For I know your frame. I created you. And I have allowed this situation to come to pass. For I use all things for good, especially the hopeless ones. That is what makes me God. For you are not.

You are my child. My chosen vessel. I have paid a great price for you.

I AM God. There is nothing too hard for me.

I've got this. And I've got you.

Lift your gaze.

I exhaled. Though my heart felt heavy, I obeyed—looked out over the water. Just beyond where the glistening waves began, a school of dolphins swam, squealing and jumping in and out of the water. I smiled despite myself. They sounded like they were laughing and playing in the surf. Their joy transfixed me.

My shoulders relaxed, and I watched them for over an hour. A supernatural sense of peace washed over me. God had given me a multi-faceted gift—confirmation of his sovereignty, validation that he is the one true God, justification of his omnipotence, and sanction of his love for me, his child.

Thankfully, it is during these faith-testing times that God never leaves us nor forsakes us (Deuteronomy 31:6, Hebrews 13:5). Those are the very times he is closest to us. During a season of suffering, the Lord gave me the words for this book. He declared, "Comfort, comfort my people, says your God" (Isaiah 40:1).

For me, even the thought of writing this book was a trial. Some people come out of the womb with the gift of writing. Their words seem to leap out onto their laptops like gazelles bounding up steep ravines, making perfect prose. That has *never* been the case for me. Writing has always been an arduous process; I even had my husband proofread my emails.

As I wrestled with God over writing this book, I stubbornly told him, "You've called the wrong person, Lord. You know I can't write. You made me." Unbelievably, he was stretching me in other areas as well. He was telling me to run, something I was never good at. In school, maintaining some sort of cardiovascular strength for sports was always a necessary evil. Now in my late-forties, I felt the Lord was telling me run *and* to write—two activities I absolutely abhorred.

In grumbling obedience, I ran. Eventually I could run a mile, and in over a year, five miles—which for me was nothing short of epic. Then one day as I started one of my long five-mile runs, I prayed for the Lord to bless it. This time, I heard him say to me, "I want you to add a mile to your run today."

I stopped stretching. "Wow, that would be six miles—a 10K! Well, Lord, you made this body and you know its limits."

In compliant faith, I ran the entire distance easily. Afterward, I praised and thanked God in stunned disbelief, telling him (as if he didn't already know), "I have never run that far before. That's a 10K! Thank you, Lord, for the strength and endurance to run six miles. I've never been a runner before."

Then he clearly said, "You've never written a book before either."

Stunned, I hung my head with the conviction of his reprimand heavy on my heart, and walked home.

The Lord had me continue to add more miles, and before I knew it, I was training for a half-marathon—13.1 miles! During one of my long training runs, I cried out to God, "Lord, I'm so tired. Can I just skip this mile-long loop?"

Gently, he said, "There are no shortcuts, my beloved. You can't truncate the process." I knew God was also referring to weariness from my trial, for he knew my heart. His words resonated deep in my soul. I chewed on them as a child works a piece of bubble gum.

> "There are no shortcuts, my beloved. You can't truncate the process."
> ~ God

No matter how difficult it is, we can't shorten our times of suffering either. We must take each step, each day, and each trial in full measure, even though the length is indeterminable. Afflictions must run their course; we need to allow for the ebb and flow of their pain. We can't water them down or skip them, no matter how agonizing they are. The encouraging and sometimes forgotten realization is that they're only for a season. They do eventually pass, we just don't know when. Unfortunately, trials don't come with expiration dates.

Even with these revelations, I still struggled with the Lord's directive to write. I continued to cry out to him. I felt like a kindergartner having a tantrum and stomping her feet instead of just sitting down to obediently tie her shoes.

I stubbornly told God, "Lord, you created me in my mother's womb. You made me to swim like a duck, not to climb trees like a squirrel or write a book. I think you called the wrong person."

> Trials don't come with expiration dates.

God was silent.

My moaning continued, "God, you're asking me to do the impossible, like having a duck climb a tree." Dejected and full of self-pity, I prayed. As I cried out to him, I saw a picture of a flourishing coconut tree with large, deep green palm leaves. The tree had grown parallel to the ground and this duck was happily waddling up the trunk, quacking loudly all the way.

The Lord spoke to my heart, "See, I can even make trees grow crooked to accomplish my will."

Apparently, there is no point in arguing with an omnipotent, all-powerful God.

So I acquiesced to become both a writer and a runner, and it was during those long training runs, when it was just the rhythmic sound of my feet pounding against the pavement, that I most clearly heard from God. It seemed after I humbled myself, stopped telling God what I wanted him to do, and just listened, I was finally comforted. Those revelations I received while running were my personal lifeline and the fodder for this book.

Instead of turning from God, I pressed in even harder. I prayed that if God would not lift this trial from us, then he would give me the grace to endure. Now, after completing my second 26.2-mile marathon and finishing this book, I am once again awed by God.

This book is the fruit of my obedience to become one of God's scribes. And if God can use me, he can use you. It seems that God uses those who have gone through the flames of affliction to go back and pour water on those still going through the fire.

> It seems that God uses those who have gone through the flames of affliction to go back and pour water on those still going through the fire.

It is my hope this book will lift your gaze to God as you're going through times of suffering. For clarity, I have divided the book into four sections on trials: the nature of trials, the reasons for them, our response to them, and our greatest need. Each chapter includes several gems: topical biblical stories with present-day applications; supporting prophetic words/poems; my heartfelt intercessory prayers for the readers of this book, followed by application questions; and a prayer journal to apply God's Word to your situation.

In my opinion, the prophetic words and my prayers for you, the reader, are the sweetest and most encouraging portions of the book. These are the bright red bow on the biblical truths in each chapter. They are confirmation that our struggles are real, hard, and faith-challenging, and that God is not deaf to our cries. This book can be used individually or in a group setting. You can dive as deep as you want into the bottomless sea of God's love. Allow time to pause, reflect, and apply the Word of God to your life. Let God's words heal, comfort, and give you peace.

If you do decide to go through this book in a group setting, please be sensitive to others and do not share someone else's pain. Before you're tempted to share what someone else has said, ask yourself, *Am I part of the problem or solution?* If you're not part of the solution, then you don't have permission to repeat what they've said. You want to establish and maintain a confidential foundation for your group. It needs to be a safe place for everyone to share. Start each gathering with prayer. Ask the Holy Spirit to meet all of you, guard against gossip, and comfort you as you read and apply his Word to your life.

God is a miracle worker. Sometimes he answers prayers in ways we would never imagine. As a suggestion, when God answers your prayers, date and write them in the prayer journal section in red or another color. Journaling and recording God's responses to our prayers fans the flames of our faith, especially when we go back and reread them. It's encouraging to see how an awesome, all-powerful, and transcendent God loves us enough to not only hear our prayers but also answer them as well!

I pray this book is a source of comfort for you or someone you love. As the words in this book have comforted me and brought me closer to God, it is my prayer that you experience the same. Draw close to him and allow God, through his Word, to completely envelope you in his loving, protective arms. He made you, formed your innermost being, and only he can console you in ways you never imagined possible.

Lift your gaze, my friend.

Lift your gaze.

CHAPTER ONE

Lift Your Gaze

Even though I walk through the valley of the shadow of death, I will *fear no evil, for you are with me*; your rod and your staff, they comfort me. You prepare a table before me in the presence of my enemies; you anoint my head with oil; my cup overflows. Surely goodness and mercy shall follow me all the days of my life, and *I shall dwell in the house of the* LORD *forever.*

~ PSALM 23:4–6 *emphasis mine*

THOSE WORDS WERE hard to swallow, especially today. My breathing was labored. I was terrified. In an attempt for serenity, I went for a run. A wall of humidity greeted me. It was like breathing through a wet rag.

I ran slowly, methodically, trying to propel my body through the thick, sticky mist. My legs were not cooperating. They felt like they were incased in cement. My heart was fearful, and with nothing else left of my physical strength, I prayed, "God, just tell me what to do."

We had moved to Florida from Delaware a few weeks earlier, and the mother-of-all-hurricanes, Irma, was barreling down on the state of Florida like a huge boot sole over an ant. Wind speeds were estimated at over 185 miles per hour. I had never driven that fast and had no concept of what we or our house would be like after being hit with winds or objects that flew through the air at that speed.

The power company called with terse yet automated messages. We were told to prepare for being without electricity for a minimum of a week during a sweltering-hot summer. Translation: no air conditioning, no refrigeration, no lights, and no cable television for updates. The meteorologists on The Weather Channel spewed out hurricane facts like an overheated computer. The entire state was told to brace for "catastrophic" devastation. Our area was told not to evacuate, but to hunker down, board up our windows, seal all our personal belongings (especially photos and framed prints) in double plastic trash bags with duct tape, and wait out the storm in an interior room padded with mattresses.

Running that day did nothing to calm my nerves. My husband, a former longtime Florida resident, was away on a business trip. He would return right before the tempest was expected to hit our area. Just recently unpacked from our move to the state, I was attempting to prepare for a hurricane alone with our precocious six-year-old. People hoarded bottled water, canned food, and gasoline. The lines at the grocery stores were at least ten carts long, blocking all the aisles, and most gas stations were out of fuel.

Sometimes, despite our effort, we know we're about to enter "the valley of the shadow of death" and yet there is nothing we can do about it. We know it's going to be disastrous, yet God in his sovereignty has ordained for us to ride out the storm. He is telling us to be still and trust him (Psalm 46:10). Those words were too difficult for me to comprehend right now though. And running provided little to no solace during the chaos.

Still running, I again prayed, "Lord, just tell me what to do. Do I buy a generator? Do I ignore the warnings and flee with my son? Just speak, my God. Your servant is listening."

The response?

Silence.

Then I saw it, and the image was breathtaking.

I saw a huge hand. My husband, son, and I were placed gently in its enormous palm. The hand closed, protecting my family from the storm. Despite the fierce wind, pelting rain, and angry swirling tornadoes, we were protected by the shielding hand of God. After the tempest passed, the massive hand slowly opened and we emerged completely unscathed from the wrath of the storm. We were dazed and amazed at the destruction and devastation around us yet were in awe of the level of fortification bestowed upon us.

Then I heard it: "I take care of and uphold my children, even in the midst of the storm." I stopped running and a tear of gratitude slid down my cheek.

Despite the heat, humidity, and generalized societal trauma of an impending mother-of-all-hurricanes approaching, I felt the peace of God. I received and embedded the revelation in my heart. "He's got this. He's got us. He's not going to remove the storm; he's going to protect and uphold us." I exhaled out.

As my pastor once said, "God either calms the storm or calms the child." This time, as I lifted my gaze to God, he calmed me, his child.

> "I take care of and uphold my children, even in the midst of the storm."
>
> ~ God

Some time ago, during another trial, a person asked me why my situation was so traumatic for me. He brushed off my pain like a housefly at a picnic. I smiled sympathetically at his response and told him that was one of the very premises of this book. Trials are unique, just like each person. And because each one is distinct, we all respond differently. There are no exact replicas of any storm or person, just resemblances. An incident or circumstance that derails one person's world may not elicit even a blink for another.

Sometimes trials don't pass quickly like a hurricane; they linger for far too long. And when our world is shaken repeatedly, everything we know and hold dear is irrevocably changed.

Even if we believe in God, we can start to question the allowance of such intense continued pain. We might wonder, *Is God* really *on my side?* and *How can a good God allow* this *to happen?* or *What did I do to deserve* this?

Sometimes we can get stuck in a loop, repeating the memory of when the trial first began. We distinctly remember *that* day when our life completely derailed. We even fool ourselves that if we'd responded differently, that could have altered the outcome.

Despite the specifics of the cause of the trial or storm, two things remain the same: they are hard, and our emotional and spiritual states are extremely volatile and unpredictable. Our emotions are like a bouncing ping-pong ball in a cement room—they're all over the place. On some days we just glide through life so easily that people around us have no idea of the magnitude of insanity swirling around us. Other days we're barking at everyone, feeling like we're trudging through quicksand and wondering if this will ever end. And just when as we think we're doing a decent job of keeping everything together, we come unhinged and dissolve into a crying mess or explode into a fit of anger in the grocery store.

Unfortunately, some of us can also get trapped in the darkness. The initial pain from the cold, hard, and empty place of self-isolation has started to become familiar. It now sadly has evolved into a false sense of security. We receive comfort from the pain. Perhaps we rest firmly in the false belief that our God has left us. We woefully trudge through life, leaving a trail of dismay behind us. We wear our trial like a badge of courage and dominate every conversation with it by dramatically swinging it up on the table with a loud, resounding thud. Surrounded by the deep waters of depression and hopelessness, we fear that those very waters that once isolated us and comforted us from the pain are about to pull us down to a depth that we will never emerge from.

Trials also create a desperate craving for comfort. In a feeble attempt for consolation, we can turn to outlets like social media only to find everyone else is living a life of rainbows, unicorns, and cupcakes. Or we can turn to other vices to medicate the pain, like food, sex, alcohol, or drugs. After the initial taste, these idols leave us feeling even more empty.

God only prunes the fruitful, and he uses trials to do it. Even as he is expertly and mercifully removing the old, he gives us enough grace to endure the pruning. The act of removing the unnecessary is usually the most painful part. We want to hold on to the very things that have provided solace in the past but are no longer useful—like a comfortable yet worn-out old sweater full of holes. We don't even realize the things we use for relief are the very things that imprison us. God has better things in store than false security blankets; he wants us to ascend to higher heights, trusting in him completely.

God only prunes the fruitful, and he uses trials to do it.

As we emerged from that hurricane, I felt like God had trimmed the entire state of Florida. All the dead leaves, branches, and trees without a strong and deep root system were demolished and removed. Only the clean, green, lush foliage remained. Likewise, sometimes God uses trials or hurricanes in our lives to remove all the lifeless, unusable, and obstructive idols that unknowingly impede our spiritual growth.

Trials can also make us feel like we're suffocating. We need the influx of God's Spirit so desperately that our bodies crave it. Some of us can become too saturated in self-pity and anguish to even begin to lift our gaze. And we can forget that "in all things God works for the good of those who love him, who have been called according to his purpose" (Romans 8:28 NIV).

But sometimes our trials or storms last for years or even decades, like times in the wilderness. Those long-lasting ones can be the hardest to endure and are the easiest way to lose our faith.

The two million Israelites had that same crisis of faith as they wandered through the wilderness for forty years after they escaped bondage in Egypt. They seemed just like me: daily fearful of the unknown, looking back to the oppression of slavery with rose-colored glasses, and desperately wanting some solace from normalcy.

These Israelites, like me before Christ, were delivered from a life of barbaric servitude, but still yearned for the security of captivity that Egypt provided. They had structure in Egypt, living in homes and eating vegetables and fruit they grew in their own gardens. They were also cruelly beaten and forced into backbreaking manual labor with limited resources. Their male children were heartlessly slaughtered at birth. All because the ruler of Egypt at that time, Pharaoh, saw their strength in numbers and the fruit of their anointing as God's chosen race. He feared them and made their life in Egypt excruciating.

Despite the evil swirling around them, God delivered them through the faith of one man, Moses. God placed the Israelites in the wilderness to grow them, stretch them, and change their mind-sets from that of a slave to that of a warrior. This process needed time—forty years' worth of time, to be exact.

God *was* and *is* a bondage-breaker. He does the same for us during our trials, storms, and times in the wilderness. He breaks the bondage of the lies of slavery in our life, making us free. Unfortunately, this process usually takes longer and is more painful than we'd like.

Our times in the wilderness are so hard for us because our focus is on the gift, not the giver. God supernaturally provided the Israelites food each day, called *manna* or "bread from heaven." He did this for forty years! Manna was a white substance like coriander seed and tasted like wafers made with honey (Exodus 16:31). It was a gift from God, presented to them every morning for six days a week.

God *was* and *is* a bondage-breaker.

His instructions were clear: They were to gather only what they needed for themselves and their family for that day. On the sixth day, they were provided a double portion so they could rest on the seventh day, the Sabbath. If they tried to save any for the next day on any other day, it would become filled with worms and rot (Exodus 16:20).

Manna, God's sustenance, is like grace. God only gives us enough for each day. "Sufficient for the day is its own trouble" (Matthew 6:34), and sufficient for today is its own grace. We can't store manna or grace. Neither one keeps. Each day we receive our daily portion. In doing so, we must lift our gaze in gratitude to God, the giver, and not to the gift.

For the Israelites during their time in the wilderness, God had them depend on him for everything, even which direction daily to walk. That level of dependency was essential for their growth as warriors. It was probably the most terrifying part of the wilderness—trusting God for *everything*. It must have been very humbling. I would have had repeated meltdowns.

Our times in the wilderness are so hard for us because our focus is on the gift, not the giver.

Even though God provided every day for the Israelites in the wilderness, they didn't appreciate it, and sometimes we don't either. God allows us to experience the fruit of our self-sufficiency to bring us to our darkest hour so that we, like the Israelites, cry out only to him. It is during those times we wonder where God has been during our time of suffering. Mercifully, he is there, actively protecting us from something far worse. Those are the very moments when God is gently moving us out of our pain.

These trials, storms, and afflictions in the wilderness that God allows in our lives are the perfect soil for a miracle. Those times when no hope exists for anything in the natural are the times when his grace is the sweetest. We sense God's presence drawing close to us. He opens those eternal floodgates of love, and we feel his breath upon us, giving us fresh wind—just like he gave me that picture of him upholding my family in his hand during the hurricane. Those sweet moments of grace give us the power to focus squarely on the giver, our God.

The joy we once had is ours again! That joy is based on the posture of our hearts, not the situation. The trial, storm, or wilderness may still be present, but our perspective, or rather our heart, has changed. We are now focused on God, for whatever we focus on gets bigger.

Let me restate that: *Whatever we focus on gets bigger.*

> Manna, God's sustenance, is like grace. God only gives us enough for each day.

Just like Peter walking on water toward his God during the storm, if we take our eyes off God during our trial, we will also sink (Matthew 14:22–23).

Thankfully, God is always there for us, pulling us back up, refocusing our gaze. If we are singularly focused on our trials, our trials get bigger than God. If we lift our gaze and look to our God instead of our trials, our God becomes bigger. When we, like Peter, see our God is greater than our time of suffering and comprehend our God is stronger than our deep waters, then we will experience the peace that transcends all human understanding even though the waves and wind continue to roar around us.

There is hope for all of us in our season of trials. It may not come in a little package with a pretty bow around it as we imagined. Maybe God doesn't remove the trial, storm, or time in the wilderness; perhaps he only provides an outpouring of his living waters and the grace to endure it.

We are his precious possession, and even though we're being brought through the purifying fires of a trial, we are loved. The Lord is the God of the living. He is the God of restoration.

We *can* experience the fullness of his joy during a time of suffering—a joy that transcends our situation. And this joy is not idol-induced, but rather God-induced. When our Creator permeates us with his Spirit, especially during a trial, there is no other earthly experience that can compare. Sometimes, as we are struggling through a trial and when we have lost our joy and hope, even our closest friends and trusted counselors can't rescue us from our deep waters. During these times we need to turn to our Creator, the one who knows every

> Whatever we focus on gets bigger.

cell in our bodies. He knows our frame and every function of it. He alone is the best candidate to perform our much-needed spiritual tune-up or complete overhaul.

My prayer is that you would feel his closeness and tenderness. Through immersing yourself in his Word, the Holy Bible, and through prayer, he will comfort you. Again, he might not deliver you from your situation, but he will console you.

The anointing that comes so freely from the depths of his grace will completely cover you. Only he possesses the most powerful healing tool ever known to man: his love. God loves us so much that he gave up his most treasured possession for us: his one and only Son.

You may have never heard about God's son, Jesus Christ, who came to die for you. He paid the penalty in full for all your sins on the barbaric instrument of Roman torture, the cross. The very thing you crave and are searching for—God's love—is only accessible through the sacrificial death Jesus endured. That love is the very elixir from our Creator that is so freely given to all who still feel empty despite the false promises of this world.

If that is you, then the Lord God, your Creator, would want you to call out to him in prayer and ask him for his help. Pray aloud or to yourself:

> Lord, I need you. I am a sinner. I am not perfect. I have done things that I wish I hadn't. I need you, Jesus, in my heart. Fill me with your presence through your Holy Spirit. I repent of my sins and declare you, Jesus Christ, as my personal Savior.

By praying this prayer, you have confessed with your mouth that Jesus Christ is Lord and has died for you. You have repented of your sins. You have now placed your faith in Jesus as your personal Savior, and are reconciled with your Creator, your holy and perfect God. My prayer for you is as you open your heart to Jesus, you finally feel fulfilled and are immersed in the amazing love that comes so freely from God through his Holy Spirit.

Despite the trials, storms, and times in the wilderness that God has lovingly permitted to permeate my life, solely by his grace I rebound back to truth: God will work *all* things for good, including this trial. God has called me according to his purpose. God is using my trials to force me to draw closer to him. This book is the fruit of Romans 8:28 in my life.

So I made a choice. I prayed again.

This time God spoke.

And oh, did he speak…

Lift Your Gaze

Why are you so downcast, my beloved? Am I not the God of seeing?

I see your affliction! I see you! I see your trials! Am I not the God of hearing? I hear your groans. Am I not the God of creation? Didn't I create the world and everything in it? Am I not the God of the universe? Didn't I create the stars, the moon, the sun, and all the planets? Am I not a *big*

God? Am I not your God? Didn't I send my one and only Son to save you? Didn't he pay the price for your sins, so you will not perish in hell but instead have eternity with *me*?

Is anything too hard for ME? Am I not the God of all flesh? Have I not created you? Don't I know your frame? Don't I see your pain? Your weaknesses? Your frailness? Don't I keep every one of your tears in a bottle?

Despite what you feel, I AM close to you. Have I ever left you or forsaken you?

Am I not larger, stronger, more amazing, and more awesome than your trials?

I AM immutable, omnipresent, omnipotent, omniscient, and unwavering in my steadfast love, care, and provision for you. Again, I have *never* left you nor forsaken you.

Lift your gaze, my child! Look to the God who has saved you. Look to me, the God who allowed his only Son to die for your transgressions, so you can have sweet communion and eternal life with me.

Therefore, I cannot and will not withhold any good gift from you. For I have not withheld my only Son as propitiation for your sins. I have done this so you can boldly approach my throne of grace. Come to me. Come and see. Taste and see. Feel my grace. Be overcome with my love. Inhale my Holy Spirit. Ignite those fires that once burned so bright for me. Forgive those who have sinned against you, as I have forgiven you. Remember, ALL things work together for good to those who love me and are called according to my purposes. And that would be you. You are my chosen one, my child, my bride, and the one I have paid the highest price for; I have paid your ransom in full! For I have bought you for a great price, the price of my Son's life.

You are redeemed from the payment of your sins! Your debt has been paid! You are justified. You are mine. By your faith in Jesus, you have MY Holy Spirit in you. My Spirit dwells in you. He is your helpmate. He is your comforter.

Lift your gaze to where your help comes from.

Lift your gaze to your God.

For I am *your* God.

I have created the heavens and the earth.

I have saved you and redeemed you.

You are saved.

You are mine.

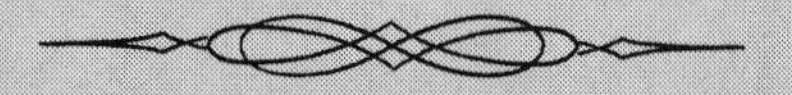

Be encouraged. Your God sees you and holds you during your time of suffering. Perhaps just the confirmation that God loves you is enough. Maybe the truth that he wants to reach out to touch your heart, uphold you, and bless you is all the consolation you need.

Whatever the posture of your heart, know that God is the antidote. He is so near to you, and he wants to give you more of his presence, his love, and his Spirit.

Run to him. Cry out to him. Allow him to envelope you.

He is your Father.

He is more than enough.

He is God.

In fervent prayer for someone I love deeply, I asked God to keep them from danger, evil, and suffering. God replied, "Any difficulty or trial that comes upon them will be used for their good and my glory, to make them more like my Son." Remembering the source of my strength, I exhaled, "Praise God!"

This is my prayer for you …

Dear Holy and Perfect God,

Bless those that are reading this right now, oh God. Pour out your Holy Spirit into their hearts. Meet them right where they are. Drench them in your Spirit.

Where there is fear, provide your peace. Where there is strife and bitterness, provide forgiveness. Where there is need of healing, provide supernatural deliverance.

Where there is anger, provide love. Where there is unbelief in how *big* a God you are, provide faith. Where there is frustration and impatience, provide grace. Where there is deception, provide truth. Where there is ignorance, provide wisdom. Where there is confusion, provide discernment. Fill their hearts with your healing balm, completely cover their pain. Allow your Spirit to come into their hearts in a deeper way; minister to their souls in a way that only *you* can. Help them lift their gaze to you, a holy and perfect God who loves them so much that you gave your only Son's life as payment for their sins so they can be reconciled with you, a holy and perfect God.

Become their God. Become *bigger* in their eyes, *bigger* than their trials.

Lift their gaze to you, oh Lord. Have them fix their eyes on you, oh God.

You are an amazing God. You are our God, our Father, our Kinsman Redeemer, and our *everything.* Have them develop a supernatural love and need of your Word found only in the Holy Bible. Live in them. Dwell in them. Pour out your peace into them. Let the world see your Spirit in them. Mark them with your Spirit as children of a holy God.

In Jesus' precious name, I pray.

Amen.

APPLICATION QUESTIONS

Getting to the Heart of It

"Behold, I am the LORD, the God of all flesh. *Is anything too hard for me?*"
~ JEREMIAH 32:27 *emphasis mine*

Reread the verse above. Digest it in your heart: *Nothing is too hard for God* (Jeremiah 32:27). He is abundantly able to bless you. Rest assured that he hears you, knows you, and is working all things out for good (Romans 8:28) despite what it might look or feel like.

Answer these application questions honestly. Keep them to yourself or share them in a group. Either way, be encouraged. God is for you.

1. To help you turn to God as you process your current or previous trial, difficult situation, and/or season of suffering, write down a few sentences describing your storm.

2. What is the first thing you think about each day when you wake up? God or your trial? Why?

3. What would focusing on God each day instead of your trial look like in your life?

4. Create a daily action plan of at least three things you can do to turn your thoughts to God instead of your trial.

1

2

3

5. Do you believe God can give you peace and joy during your time of suffering? Why or why not?

6. What if God chooses *not* to end this season but to continue it. What would your response be? Why?

7. Give three specific examples of how God has been faithful in times past.

   1

   2

   3

8. List the names of three people whom you can ask to pray for you.

   1 ______________________________

   ____

   2 ______________________________

   ____

   3 ______________________________

   ____

9. What will you ask them to pray for you?

   ____

   ____

   ____

   ____

   ____

   ____

   ____

   ____

   ____

   ____

   ____

Prayer Journal

"*Ask and it will be given to you; Seek and you will find; Knock and the door will be opened to you.* For everyone who asks receives; the one who seeks finds; and to the one who knocks, the door will be opened. Which of you, if your son asks for bread, will give him a stone? Or if he asks for a fish, will give him a snake? *If you, then, though you are evil, know how to give good gifts to your children, how much more will your Father in heaven give good gifts to those who ask him!*"

~ Matthew 7:7–11 NIV *emphasis mine*

1. Before presenting your prayer requests to God, remind yourself of who God is. List five of God's attributes that resonate with you (such as all-powerful, all-present, all-knowing, holy, without the confines of time, almighty, majestic, beautiful, etc.).

   1 ____________________
   2 ____________________
   3 ____________________
   4 ____________________
   5 ____________________

2. List at least five blessings in your life that you are grateful for.

   1 ____________________
   2 ____________________
   3 ____________________
   4 ____________________
   5 ____________________

3. List your prayer requests.

4. Write down anything else the Lord is speaking to your heart.

5. Finally, worship God to remind yourself of what an awesome God he is. And praise him in advance for whatever the outcome.

CHAPTER TWO

Why Me?

Beloved, do not be surprised at the fiery ordeal among you, which comes upon you for your testing, as though some strange thing were happening to you; but to the degree that you share the sufferings of Christ, keep on rejoicing; so that also at the revelation of his glory, you may rejoice with exultation. If you are reviled for the name of Christ, *you are blessed, because the Spirit of glory and of God rests upon you*. Therefore, let those also who suffer according to the will of God entrust their souls to a faithful Creator in doing what is right.

~ 1 PETER 4:12–13, 19 NASB *emphasis mine*

"SERIOUSLY?" I MUTTERED, looking up at the dark cloud overhead through the pouring rain pelting me in the face. We were in the middle of a torrential downpour … on the beach … in the middle of the summer. It had rained earlier in the day, and the weather report said we'd have sunshine for the next few hours. Wrong. The once-crowded beach was now pretty empty. I looked to the left, and no one was on the beach and it wasn't raining, not even a drop. To my right, the sand wasn't even wet as far as my eyes could see.

I was incensed. Not a rain cloud in the sky, except over where we stood. This dark, foreboding cloud hovered above in a one-hundred-yard radius, wringing out its contents where we had just set up our blanket. We pathetically huddled under our beach umbrella, soaking wet.

I shook my fist upward. "Come on, God! I mean really? Rain on *just* us?"

God was silent. I heard nothing. Just the sound of big fat rain drops hitting the thick vinyl umbrella.

I sighed.

My husband's eyes narrowed in frustration as he looked at me. He disliked the beach and despised being wet even more.

"Well, it's only one cloud," I offered up as a consolation. "It'll pass soon."

He glared harder at me.

Miraculously, as soon as the rain started, it stopped. We emerged from our umbrella shelter, relieved.

As we reset our beach camp and spread out our blanket, I was glad we decided to wait out the rain. The beach was now pristine, newly cleaned by the rain, and empty. We made sand castles and played in the surf.

Then I looked up and stopped. My bright green plastic shovel slipped from my hand.

A brilliant full rainbow emerged over the ocean, each end touching the sea. Its colors were incredibly vibrant and intense, framed on top by thick angry-gray clouds and underneath by soft white wisps of paint on a sky-blue canvas. The light brown divots in the sand set off the idyllic colors beautifully.

I was awestruck. "Wow," was all I could whisper as I ran back to our beach bag and dug out my phone. I fumbled with it, trying desperately not to get it wet or sandy as I attempted to capture it in panoramic pictures. "Thanks, God."

Then I heard it. He spoke tenderly yet firmly to my heart, "The greater the storm, the greater the blessing."

Smiling, I nodded.

Sometimes the trials are just for us. It can be hard to trust God while we're immersed in an angry tempest and everyone else around us seems to be reveling in their blessings. I assume that since I'm a good person, I therefore deserve good things—not trials, even though they might eventually end with a blessing. I want world peace and acts of random kindness to abound like popcorn popping at the movie theater. I want heaven on earth. Instead, conflicts seem to proliferate and dominate my life.

And it's not just in my little world—it's everywhere. Horrific atrocities of starvation, natural disasters, looting, malnourishment, rapes, child abuse, suicides, murders, genocides, and bombings dominate our newsfeed. Even though we live in a fallen world inhabited by sinful people, I still cry out to God, "Why is life so hard? Lord, you are in control. You don't *need* to use trials. You are so big that you could just teach us during our joyful times."

And like a child, I continue my self-righteous tirade with, "Haven't I tried to walk in a worthy manner? Don't I try to follow you and obey you? You could have changed this. Why didn't you? And why *me*?"

Then I dejectedly slump to a pile on the floor and sigh. After all, God is sovereign. Yes, he could have altered the situation and made things easier (or worse) but elected not to. He orchestrated all these events for my good and his glory (Romans 8:28).

> "The greater the storm, the greater the blessing."
>
> ~ God

Then I wonder, what if I changed my "Why me?" to "Why not me?" Why do I inaccurately assume God owes me or anyone else a trial-free life? The propaganda that believing in God exempts us from trials is a very tempting idol. I didn't receive a "Get Out of Trials Free" card when I became a Christian. Did you?

The funny thing is, never does the Bible, God, or Jesus promise that life will be easy or equitable. The Bible states quite the opposite. It's very clear, trials *must* come; there is no *if* but a *when*. Jesus confirms it when he states that the "Son of man *must* suffer many things. … If anyone would come after me, let him deny himself and take up his cross daily and follow me" (Luke 9:22–23 emphasis mine). And "'We *must* go through many hardships to enter the kingdom of God'" (Acts 14:22 NIV emphasis mine).

The Message version of the Bible offers further clarity on Jesus' teaching:

> "Anyone who intends to come with me has to let me lead. You're not in the driver's seat; I am. *Don't run from suffering; embrace it.* Follow me and I'll show you how. Self-help is no help at all. *Self-sacrifice is the way, my way, to finding yourself, your true self.* What kind of deal is it to get everything you want but lose yourself? What could you ever trade your soul for?" (Matthew 16:24–26 MSG emphasis mine)

Those verses gave me pause. Sometimes I'm so absorbed in the difficulties of today that I forget the glorious promises of eternity. If

I was to measure all the atrocities I have faced and weigh them against all the wonderful things in my life, I would humbly realize that my life is nowhere near fair. I am blessed beyond measure compared to a quarter of world's population. Having traveled to portions of the world that don't even have clean running water, adequate sewage systems, or electricity,[1] I find my heart quickly melts from selfish entitlement to selfless gratitude.

> I didn't receive a "Get Out of Trials Free" card when I became a Christian. Did you?

Unfortunately, whether we like it or not, trials are unavoidable during our lifetime. In hindsight, it seems we learn the most during our unescapable times of suffering. Trials are our greatest teachers. For me, the most interesting part is that God, in his infinite wisdom, allows us to be tested. We must decide if we will be a receptive or defiant student. And God is usually the quietest when we are going through a trial—just like a teacher giving a test and waiting to see if we'll apply what we have learned.

Isaac Newton elaborates:

> Trials are medicines which our gracious and wise Physician prescribes because we need them; and he proportions the frequency and weight of them to what the case requires. Let us trust his skill and thank him for his prescription.[2]

Isn't that so true? God is all-wise and all-knowing. He knows what's best for us. Even as I reflect upon the tapestry of my life and recall when I felt like I was spiritually drowning, I now realize in hindsight, those were the times when I grew the most. In my wildest dreams, I couldn't have imagined how God would use my seemingly horrific times for good. I couldn't lift my gaze. I was embroiled in the moment. My tempest dominated my every thought and action, and even infiltrated my prayer life.

During one of my difficult times, I remember questioning God with "Why me?" and praying:

> God, I know you are going to use my trial for good. And I know that you are sovereign and don't waste anything. And you know my tears—you keep them in a bottle. God, I know you will produce good, healthy fruit in my life. But I am weary. I need you to pour out your grace upon me to give me the strength to endure this trial. Bless me with the patience to get out of your way and allow you to work all things out for good in your perfect timing, not mine. I need you to bestow upon me the patience, wisdom, and discernment to wait to see the fruit that will come from this trial. Please provide confirmation in the flesh that you will not waste this suffering. Use it for your good. Produce something amazing from it.

God is faithful. He answered my prayer immediately. Right after I finished, the phone rang. It was a friend whom I'd unexpectedly ran into at a recent conference. She wanted to thank me for sharing the gospel with her. She now had joy in her life because she'd accepted Jesus as her personal Savior after one of our conversations.

My friend then expressed her gratitude for the source of my trial: an angry third party who refused to allow me to attend the same event closer to home. She reminded me that had this person been reasonable, I would have missed an opportunity to reconnect with her and introduce her to Jesus. My friend will now spend eternity in heaven with Jesus because the Lord allowed me to experience the repercussions of someone's sin. He used their rage for good and his glory.

God *is* big enough to work good from evil. He repeatedly does this.

Consider Queen Esther, the main character in one of my favorite stories in the Bible. I'm sure she questioned God when she was faced with the choice of death or her entire race being annihilated.

Just to give you some background, Esther was Jewish and born in Persia, a foreign pagan land. Her name in Hebrew was Hadassah, which "means 'myrtle,' a tree whose leaves only release their fragrance when crushed."[3] The same is accurate for us; our true scent emerges only when we are being squeezed. During a trial, what aroma do you emit? Mine isn't always pleasant. Do you elicit the sweet smell of the love of Christ or the stench of anger and bitterness? Unfortunately, I tend to lean to the latter, especially if I am physically drained.

Hadassah produced a bouquet of boldness and faith when she was being tested. Even though her parents died when she was young, she was steeped in strong Jewish traditions by her Uncle Mordecai. During their exile in Babylon, the Hebrew people questioned God's provision and care, and their faith.[4] Then she was abruptly removed from safety and protection from her uncle and placed in the king's harem. Her uncle, understanding the times and prejudice against the Jews, told her to conceal her heritage.

In the harem, she was given a new name, Esther, which means "hidden."[5] God blessed her with favor, and she eventually became queen of Persia. When the destruction of the entire Jewish nation seemed imminently orchestrated by an evil man, Haman, her Uncle

Our true scent emerges only when we are being squeezed. During a trial, what aroma do you emit?

Mordecai challenged her to intercede on behalf of the Jews to the king of Persia.

I'm sure Esther was terrified and asked, "Why me?" as she responded to her uncle's petition:

> "All the king's servants and the people of the king's provinces know that if any man or woman goes to the king inside the inner court without being called, there is but one law—to be put to death, except the one to whom the king holds out the golden scepter so that he may live. But as for me, I have not been called to come in to the king these thirty days." (Esther 4:11)

I'm sure the Holy Spirit pierced her heart as her uncle firmly replied like a father chastising a child, instead of a subject responding to his queen:

> "For if you keep silent at this time, relief and deliverance will rise for the Jews from another place, but you and your father's house will perish. *And who knows whether you have not come to the kingdom for such a time as this?*" (Esther 4:14 emphasis mine)

Amid her time of testing, she forcibly lifted her gaze to God and prayed. Esther stopped asking "Why me?" and sought God. I envisioned Esther with a new gleam in her eyes, shoulders now squared and her jaw set as she instructed her uncle with faith and confidence to:

> "Go, gather all the Jews to be found in Susa, and hold a fast on my behalf, and do not eat or drink for three days, night or day. I and my young women will also fast as you do. Then I will go to the king, though it is against the law, and if I perish, I perish." (Esther 4:16)

After she and her companions fasted and prayed, Queen Esther donned her best robes and boldly went into the king's inner court without an invitation, even if it meant her death (Esther 5:1). As she entered the court, the king mercifully outstretched his golden scepter, and in doing so, he extended her grace and exonerated her (Esther 5:2), just like our God, our King in heaven, does for us.

She then passionately and very cleverly presented a banquet invitation to Haman, the mastermind behind the plot to destroy the Jews, and the king. I believe, after the food was enjoyed, she was prompted by the Holy Spirit to not share her petition to spare the Jews just yet, but to invite them both once again for another meal the following evening. Then, after the second feast, she humbly revealed her identity as a Jew and interceded for the lives of her people. Miraculously, her request was granted. The Jews were saved, and Haman the enemy of the Jews was put to death.

Queen Esther wisely chose not to wallow in her "Why me?" quagmire. Instead, she trusted God, fasted, prayed, and then acted in faith. Her bravery and confidence saved an entire nation of people from genocide.

It is during those dark times of a trial or storm that we, like Esther, can cry out to God. Even if we ask, "Why would a loving, kind Father allow something so horrible to come into my life and afflict me?" we see that God is still there. He never left us. Then we realize how desperately we need others and, most importantly, God. And like Esther, we then give outlet to our hidden source of courage and understand why God allowed this trial to enter our life: for the sole purpose to direct us to the only true source of comfort, his Son, Jesus Christ.

Even if the Lord chooses not to remove this trial, he is using it for good. Maybe we will see the fruit of our trials now on earth, or we might have to wait until eternity to witness the full consummation of our season of suffering. Either way, we must allow our hearts to experience a new depth of gratitude for all our blessings, even the little ones. We need to guard our thoughts and not allow the noise from worldly dissatisfactions to asphyxiate the serenity that comes only from God.

> Even if the Lord chooses not to remove this trial, he is using it for good.

Experiencing peace from God realigns our vision of how big he really is in our lives. Realizing that God even uses tragedies for good transcends all our understanding. This is evident with the most tragic day in history—the day when God used an utterly depraved act of injustice, an unfair execution and an act of horror, for the good of every person born. God allowed his Son to be the complete, living sacrifice for all our sins on a bloody cross on Calvary. This complete act of submission altered the entire trajectory of all humanity.

Solely through our faith in his Son, Jesus, the innocent lamb who died for our sins, we can now boldly approach the throne of grace of a holy and perfect God. The Lord now extends his scepter of grace to us exclusively through the shed blood of Jesus Christ. Like Esther, we don't receive death and damnation for the payment of our sins; instead we receive eternal life.

This is only achieved by a simple confession of faith declaring Jesus Christ as our Savior. Once uttered, we are now forgiven from the penalty of our sins. Our wrongdoings that were once as red as crimson are now washed as clean as freshly driven snow. Jesus took all our sins with him to hell and paid the price in *full*. This was done so that we, as believers in Christ, will never have to experience separation from God and the eternal consequences of our sins. Since Jesus rose from the dead on the third day after his execution, we now have sweet communion with God.

As children of God, we are not perfect—we are forgiven. The cross solidified *who* saved us: only the Lord Jesus Christ. It confirmed *what* we were saved from: the wrath of God. This gift is for all who believe Jesus died for them, as they trust in him for their salvation.

Thank you, Jesus.

Thank you, God.

Why Me?

You ask, "Why?" Why *you*, my child?
You ask, "Why now?"
You ask this from your God?

Why *not*, my child?

You tell me "It's not fair."

Was it fair for my one and only sinless Son to die for the sins of the world?

Was it fair to have his blood spilled in full payment for all humanity to cover all their sins: past, present and future?

Is it fair that my Son's righteousness is now imputed upon them?

Is it fair they are now able to approach a holy God and enjoy eternal life with their maker? Is any of that *fair*?

Have I ever promised that you would *not* have trials?

Have I ever promised that life would be easy?

Behold, I have refined you, but not as silver; I have treated you better than silver. I have tried you in the furnace of affliction. For my own sake, for my own name's sake, I did it, for how should my name be profaned? My glory I will not give to another.

How else would I be glorified if there were no trials?

I am glorified through you as you desperately seek me amid your trial.

As you do, everyone who is around you, watching you, they will see my miraculous hand at work in your life through this seemingly impossible trial.

How else would I be glorified except through your faith in me during your darkest hours? How will they know to seek me in their trials if they do not perceive you desperately seeking my face throughout your storm?

This, my child, is how I am glorified.

This is how, even now with all the sin in this world, I am glorified.

Remember the disciples in a boat? When Peter got out of the boat and walked toward me during the storm? I didn't need the storm. But the storm made him cry out to his Savior. And his faith allowed him to walk on water toward me. That's how I am glorified. I am glorified through you, just like Peter on that stormy day at sea, seeking me in the absolute darkest-point, the vortex of your trial.

You are my beacon of hope to those who are watching you, especially those who do not believe in me yet and who deny the existence of me as their Creator.

You, by running to me in your desperate hour of need, are glorifying me.

That is how the world sees that I AM the great comforter.

I AM your God. I AM your Kinsman Redeemer. I AM your hope.

I AM life and I AM as necessary to you as the very air you breathe.

I AM your Savior. I AM your provider. I AM your protector. I AM your healer.

I AM your everything, for I AM God.

I AM glorifying myself right now through you.

I AM working all things out for good in your life.

Sit back and wait.

Trust *me.*

Take a deep breath and allow the Holy Spirit to pour into your heart. I pray his peace would then overflow out of your heart. As you walk through the valley of the shadow of death and fear no evil (Psalm 23:4), this is my prayer for you:

Dear God,

Bless those who are reading this right now. Use your Holy Spirit to minister peace to their hearts. Give them confirmation in their flesh that you are an omniscient, omnipresent, omnipotent, holy, and perfect God who is working *all* things out for good, especially for them during this season of their difficulty. Give them your peace until you lift this trial.

Bless them, great King. Bless them with your favor, your joy, and your grace. Help them quickly forgive those who have sinned against them. Permit them to see that their sins against you are greater than those who have sinned against them. Allow them to see those who have sinned against them as you so mercifully do.

Oh, God, pour out your Spirit into their hearts. Heal them and remove any root of bitterness. Convict them of any unforgiveness they still harbor, dwell on, or keep buried. Help them to repent from their unforgiveness as they fix their gaze steadily on your cross. Dissolve the source of any anger, sadness, or unbelief.

Give them your peace, oh God. Be glorified in their lives.

I pray that they are like the man from Gerasenes who was once declared beyond help and without hope, but then through a single command from you, he was made whole and his spirit was peacefully quieted within him.

I pray that my dear friends who are reading this now are at peace and that the attack of the enemy is thwarted.

I pray they are no longer subjected to the bondage of negative thinking, harmful activities, and/or destructive relationships.

I pray that they no longer believe the lies of the enemy and that they are now completely clothed in your righteousness so that they are now at peace, despite their circumstances. Make them like that man in Gerasenes long ago, whose transformation was so astounding that everyone in surrounding areas was amazed and immediately followed Jesus.

Through the transforming work of Jesus Christ, bless them with a gentle spirit, while many others will be brought to a saving knowledge of Jesus as their Savior, all because of your peace you imparted upon them.

Do a mighty work, oh God.

Have them lift their gaze to you and reflect you in their actions, deeds, and words. Break any bonds that hold them from you, oh Lord.

You are our great God.

Be glorified through us as we forgive those who have hurt us or our loved ones and trust in you when you declare, "Vengeance is *mine*, I will repay."

I pray they speak the truth. I pray they declare that you are their God. Help them, oh Lord, as they cry out to you. Comfort your people. Pour out your Holy Spirit upon them.

Give them your grace to endure, your peace to calm their storms, and your favor to bless them. Fill them through your word, your Holy Bible.

Heal them, oh Lord.

Be glorified!

In Jesus' precious name, I pray.

Amen.

APPLICATION QUESTIONS

Getting to the Heart of It

In this you rejoice, though now for a little while, if necessary, you have been grieved by various trials, so that *the tested genuineness of your faith—more precious than gold that perishes though it is tested by fire*—may be found to result in praise and glory and honor at the revelation of Jesus Christ.

~ 1 Peter 1:6–7 *emphasis mine*

1. Have you ever asked God, "Why me?" or been angry with God for a season of suffering? If you have, describe. If not, explain why.

2. What fragrance are you or have you emitted during your trials or storms? One of love and the sweetness of grace and Christ, or a stench of anger and bitterness?

3. If God gives no explanation for this trial or previous ones, do you still trust him to work all things out for good? Why or why not?

4. What has God revealed to you about himself through your trials, that you can use to help others through similar trials or situations?

5. List and describe three specific ways you can lift your gaze to God during this season and trust him with the outcome.

1

2

3

6. List any Bible story or Scripture verses that remind you that God is for you and not against you during your most challenging times.

7. What attributes of God can you concentrate on to help you remember that God is for you and to lift your gaze to him? (See chapter one's application questions if you need a reminder.)

8. List three ways you can worship God despite your circumstances.

1

2

3

9. What will you do instead of wallowing in self-pity when you are tempted to ask, "Why me?"

Jesus replied, "Truly I tell you, if you have faith and do not doubt, not only can you do what was done to the fig tree, but also you can say to this mountain, 'Go, throw yourself into the sea,' and it will be done. *If you believe, you will receive whatever you ask for in prayer.*"

~ Matthew 21:21–22 *emphasis mine*

1. Before presenting your prayer requests to God, remind yourself of who God is. List five new attributes of God you haven't listed yet (such as all-powerful, all-present, all-knowing, holy, without the confines of time, almighty, majestic, beautiful, etc.).

   1 ______________________________
   2 ______________________________
   3 ______________________________
   4 ______________________________
   5 ______________________________

2. List at least five new (that you haven't listed yet) blessings in your life that you are grateful for.

   1 ______________________________
   2 ______________________________
   3 ______________________________
   4 ______________________________
   5 ______________________________

3. List your prayer requests.

4. Write down anything else the Lord is speaking to your heart.

5. Finally, praise God to remind yourself of what an awesome God he is. And praise him in advance for whatever the outcome.

CHAPTER THREE

I AM in the Fire

"When you pass through the waters, I will be with you; and when you pass through the rivers, they will not sweep over you. When you walk through the fire, you will not be burned; the flames will not set you ablaze. For I am the LORD your God, the Holy One of Israel, your Savior. … Since you are precious and honored in my sight, and because I love you, I will give people in exchange for you, nations in exchange for your life. *Do not be afraid, for I am with you."*

~ ISAIAH 43:2–5 NIV *emphasis mine*

I RUBBED MY STIFF LEGS. They were still numb. Groaning, I climbed out of my vehicle. The distance to the ground seemed like an eternity. My toes tingled as they touched the asphalt.

"I should have stayed home," I grunted as I heaved my laptop bag and purse from the car and onto my sore shoulder. I winced at the pain. Legs buckling, I grabbed the door for balance. As I squinted through the agony, it eventually subsided and I was able to walk toward the elevator.

I squared my shoulders, trying to put the morning's trauma behind me. Before breakfast I was in a crumbled, crying mess on the kitchen floor. My two Persian cats meowed and climbed all over me with concern. In between sobs, I prayed to God to take this from me. I told him, "This is too much, Lord. I can't take it anymore."

The stress from my highly competitive sales management position in an IT start-up was slowly destroying my body. I was making too much money to resign and I enjoyed the fast-paced and flamboyant lifestyle. I didn't see a way out.

After praying, I felt peace in my heart, but that still didn't remove the queasiness from my stomach. Recently, I had received several painful cortisone shots in my shoulder. The weight of my laptop bag and purse were tearing apart any good cartilage that remained.

I sighed. I was supposed to be still in bed, but I knew I had to get back in the office. Not once did I ever take a sick day or a vacation; I was always working.

Last week's doctor's visit had been traumatic. My doctor told me with grave eyes that I desperately needed *at least* a week's worth of bedrest. I took off five days, which for me was epic. Every day I lay in bed, I grew increasingly more impatient until even my twitching drove me crazy.

My already-insane work schedule had increased exponentially since I took over the management of our international sales division. I left home at 6:00 a.m. every morning and pulled in my driveway at 10:00 p.m. each night. I was on a plane to Chicago, New York, or Boston within a moment's notice several times a week. Each weekend my eyes were glued to my laptop as I worked feverishly with my sales team to explode this new start-up as a bright, shining star on the informational technology landscape.

The elevator doors opened. It was show time. I smiled and waved at everyone and ignored the shooting pains throughout my body. I wiped the perspiration off my brow as I slid into my office, then exhaled as I fell into my leather chair and started answering emails at a lightning speed. Even though I managed the sales team and reported directly to the CEO, I still had to work my old sales territory. I was their top sales rep *and* the director of worldwide sales.

The chief operating officer coolly popped his head in my office. "Can we meet in my office now?"

Still in pain, I forced a smile. "Sure, no problem. I'll be right in."

"Thanks." He gave a slight nod and lowered his eyes. I heard his khaki pants swish as he walked briskly back to his office.

I pushed myself up, wincing, and waited for my legs to engage.

Breathe, I told myself. *Just breathe.*

The air intake marginally helped. Within a few minutes, I could walk slowly to his office with a painted-on smile. I cheerfully waved at everyone intensely working on their computers. They peeped their heads out of their open cubicles like meerkats. I confidently strode on by, like a princess in a parade.

"Thanks for coming in so quickly. I really appreciate it," the COO flatly stated. He then continued without taking a breath, "Unfortunately, we're going to have to let you go."

I was stunned. "What?"

He just stared at me.

"Are you serious?" I said louder than I intended. Self-righteously, I continued, "I am the only one bringing any income to this company! I have an hour-long commute each way, and I'm always the first one in the office and the last one to leave. I jump on a plane at the snap of a finger to Anywhere, USA, and you're *letting me go*?" My voice increased in volume with each syllable.

He nervously glanced at his door, which was slightly ajar, then jumped up and closed it. He reminded me of a nervous jack rabbit.

Running his hands through his thinning dark hair, he sat down and picked up a packet of papers. "Here is your termination agreement. You need to sign them now to receive your three months' severance package. If you choose not to sign, you will not be awarded any severance. It's your choice." He slid the packet toward me.

"I'm confused," I persisted loudly. "I'm the only one bringing in sales, and, *again, you're firing me*?" I almost spat out the words.

A conversation I'd had with one of the other women in the office a few weeks ago came to mind. She had said everything in a start-up was wonderful until the funding ran out. "Then..."—she took a breath and continued sadly—"everyone turns on each other. It's a vicious time." I had dismissed her comments, thinking that would never happen here. We were all having too much fun.

He looked at me blankly and handed me a pen with trembling hands.

I glared in defiance, grabbed the pen, and signed the papers.

"I'll escort you to your office to clear out your personal belongings," he mumbled.

My smile leaked acid. "How thoughtful of you."

After he retrieved my laptop and I stuffed all my personal belongs into my now-empty laptop bag, he silently walked me to the elevator. The doors parted, and I stepped in and shook my head.

A thought suddenly came to me. They must have assumed I had been out sick due to my impinged shoulder and that I was going to file a disability claim against the company.

As the elevator doors shut with such finality, I was beyond nauseated. I never did tell them why I'd been out sick. I was pregnant and experiencing severe complications. Holding my breath, I prayed I wouldn't vomit.

I cried on the ride home. Miraculously, I was at peace. Earlier that morning, I had prayed that God would take this situation from me. He did, just not in the way I would have liked.

Unfortunately, despite our good works and heart to please God, he still makes us go through the fire (like being terminated when pregnant with no chance of being rehired), even if we've acted blamelessly. Sometimes God doesn't remove the trial as we hoped and prayed he would. Instead he guides us right into the fire.

Despite our well-meaning protests, there is nothing we can do to avoid those all-consuming flames. The blaze's aftermath leaves nothing worldly for us to cling to. The searing heat does two important things. First, it incinerates the dross in our lives—the areas where we have doubt and lack faith. Second, it forces us to go to our Father for comfort.

When we don't allow the fire to work in our hearts and we turn to demi-gods that provide temporary solace, our trials only intensify. These idols can be food, retail therapy, anger, social media, alcohol, drugs, intimacy outside of marriage, pornography, etc. The solace we once received from these idols is now reduced to dust, and we need greater quantities to medicate the pain. Once at this point, we realize all we have left is God to provide relief, and that's right where he wants us.

Fiery trials remind me of an account of three friends: Shadrach, Meshach, and Abednego (Daniel 3:22). These men were refugees in a foreign, hostile land and served a very harsh king. They were forced to eat unfamiliar food that was against their religion. Their new king renamed each one of

When we don't allow the fire to work in our hearts and we turn to demi-gods that provide temporary solace, our trials only intensify.

them after a false god. They were given exalted positions of power over the provinces of Babylon, a pagan and barbaric nation. Their faith was continually tested in a harsh, unforgiving, and anti-God kingdom. And even when they faced impending death, their faith in God remained uncompromised.

The earthly king they served erected a solid-gold statue of himself ninety feet high and nine feet wide. He required everyone, including all royalty, nobles, and appointed wise men to attend the dedication of his monument. He even enacted a new law that stated whenever music was heard in the kingdom, everyone must bow down and worship his golden image. The consequences for disobedience were severe—one was thrown alive in a fiery furnace and burned to death (Daniel 3:1–7).

These three young men—Shadrach, Meshach, and Abednego—who were of Jewish descent, made a choice. They chose to obey their God and only worship the one true God, Yahweh. They chose not to bow down to this false golden idol despite the consequences (Daniel 2:48–49). The king ordered them to be immediately burned to death, then ragefully commanded the furnace to be heated seven times hotter than normal. They were bound, still clothed in their royal garments, and then the mightiest men of the king's army thrust them into the searing furnace.

The fire shared the king's wrath. In unbridled rage, it lashed out and incinerated the soldiers that threw those very men into the fire. Meanwhile in the flames, the three men were bestowed a great gift: they supernaturally experienced God's divine protection, care, and presence. Amid the inferno, meant for evil and destruction, Jesus, the Son of God, was physically *with* them. Then (and this is my favorite part), the king's fury disintegrated as he looked inside and saw the unbelievable. The three men he ordered to be thrown in the furnace were now not only unbound and walking around, but a *fourth* man was with them in the fire. The king loudly confirmed that the fourth man looked like the *"Son of God"* (Daniel 3:25 KJV emphasis mine).

The king boldly ordered the men to come out of the oven, and only three came out. They came out unscathed—not a hair was singed, their royal robes were not burned, and they didn't even have the slightest aroma of smoke. However, the fourth person did not emerge. Jesus remained.

We can rest in confident assurance that the same Son of God who didn't depart from those flames will never desert us. Jesus, that fourth man in the furnace, is there waiting for us at the hottest point of our fire, despite how we might feel at the time.

As we know, the enemy might try to use the fire to destroy us. And God might allow for us to go into those flames so he can spiritually unbind us. Sometimes it's only the heat from a trial that can remove the bondage of unbelief from us. Then, when all the dross is burned away and God allows us to exit the flames, we emerge with a forged sense of faith, one that won't waver under the most extreme sources of heat, because we now know deep in our hearts how big our God really is.

When we experience the depth of God's precious love for us in our firestorm, only then can we begin to glimpse the great price that was paid for us on the cross. When we have nothing else except God, we are forced to trust him completely with everything: our marriage, our children, our health, our home, our car, our financial security, our reputation, our career, our business, and

Jesus, that fourth man in the furnace, is there waiting for us at the hottest point of our fire, despite how we might feel at the time.

our every being. This is the point when the soft rubber of our faith meets the hard, hot road of a trial and we see the only real source of strength and joy, Jesus Christ.

God is with us every step of the way, just so he can be glorified. In his infinite wisdom, God does not prevent us from going through trials. Rather, he sends his Son, who is no stranger to trials, to uphold us in ours. He completely covers us. The deliverance is not always physical; sometimes it's just spiritual. Only God can bestow upon us a peace that surpasses all understanding. He does this so we can stand and glorify him as the flames lick our clothing, hair, and face yet singe nothing. As we emerge thankful, without one hair being charred, our only response is worship.

As you dive into God's Word—the Holy Bible—allow the Holy Spirit to encourage you. Permit yourself to receive the love of God. Worship Jesus as your personal Savior as you joyfully revel in the gift of eternal life and let these words to penetrate your heart…

I am in the Fire

Am I not a *big* God? Is there anything you have needed that I have not provided? I have paid a great price for you. How can I forget you? How can I cast you aside? You are mine. Can a man forget his own arm that is in pain? Can he ignore his own bodily torment?

I see your tears! I hear your cries!

Each one of your tears is like a jewel to me. I treasure them. Not one of them is wasted. I have kept each one of them in a bottle. That's how precious you and your tears are to me. I know every hair on your head. I have numbered them. I know your days. Again, I have numbered them.

Behold, I AM the God of all flesh, is there anything too hard for me?

You are my child. I have paid a great price for you. How could I leave you? How could I disown you?

Do you see the holes in my hands? Look at the wounds in my feet. Place your finger in the gash in my side.

See? Your name is written on my palms! I carry your scars upon me.

That is what held me to that cross on Calvary—my great love for you. For I could have come down and avenged myself, calling upon legions of angels, but then you would not have been justified.

You would have been found guilty.

You would have been found wanting.

You would have been damned to hell for all eternity.

I loved you so much that I became wrath for you.

I did all of this so you can approach the only holy and perfect God as your own with my perfect, righteous life as your covering.

For I AM the Great I AM.

I created the universe. I created you. I created what you love. For I AM love.

Stay here under the covering of my cross. I will sustain you. You need not worry. I AM your God.

You are my chosen child. You are my bride. I AM your Father.

I AM with you in the flames. I never left the furnace.

I AM the only true source of relief you will find from your affliction.

I will never leave you nor forsake you, for I AM God.

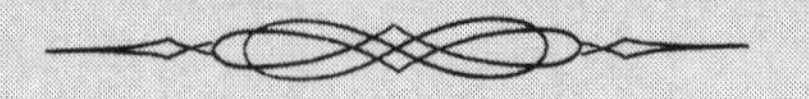

Trials subject to the flames of purification are beyond our scope of understanding. They require a level of strength we don't possess, which is why Jesus is still in those flames. We need his help to survive the combustions, lest we perish as well.

Regardless of the specific circumstances of our trial, all of us need God. He knows us better than we know ourselves. He desires a more intimate relationship with us, so we can trust him more and, in doing so, glorify him while we are still roasting in the hot trial oven:

> Anything else that can withstand *fire must be put through the fire, and then it will be clean.* But it must also be *purified with the water of cleansing.* And whatever cannot withstand fire must be put through that water. (Numbers 31:23 NIV emphasis mine)

As you sit at God's feet and engage him, find comfort that he already knows your needs. God knows what you're facing right now. Take a deep breath and rest in him during your trial. Feel the depth of his love for you. Immerse yourself in your loving, omniscient, omnipotent, omnipresent, and transcendent God who will not withhold one good thing from you, including the life of his son, Jesus Christ.

Find peace in the wisdom that if you had the same viewpoint as God and you could see what he sees, hear what he hears, and know what he knows—*you wouldn't change a thing.* You wouldn't shorten this trial. And you would completely trust in your wise, holy, perfect God.

This is my hope and prayer for you …

Dear God,

Bless those who are reading this right now. Impress upon them the deep and unfathomable love you have for them; allow them to see how precious they are to you. Let them know how much you treasure them.

Bestow upon them the simple knowledge of how you skillfully created them—delicately yet perfectly forming them in their mother's womb. Remind them they are yours and they are created in your image.

Impress upon them the deep love you have for them, a love so powerful that you gave up the life of your son, Jesus Christ, to become their personal Savior.

Pour out your life-giving knowledge into them. Become life to them. Breathe on them. As they inhale you deeply, instill in them a great love for your Word, your Holy Bible. Bless them as they daily read and devour your Word as a starving person would gulp down water and inhale succulent food.

Speak your truth to them like fresh, clean, spring air. Somehow through this trial, impart upon them the truth that you are right there with them, amid their fire, and give them your peace.

Remind them that you will never abandon them. Help them lift their gaze to their God, their Savior, and their Redeemer. Open their eyes wider so they see your hand at work in their lives. Allow them to see how big you really are. Give them divine knowledge of you, their God. Oh God, become more amazing in their eyes and their lives.

Use this purifying fire to direct their gaze solely on you. Melt their bondage. Set them spiritually free. Reinforce the deliverance found only in your Word. Assure them—the fire will *not* consume them.

Use this trial for good in their life, oh God; waste *not* this trial in their life. Encourage them to clamp both arms and legs around your cross and ground them in your truth. Impart upon them the knowledge that you are an on-time God.

You are never early and you are never late. Hear their cries, Adonai. Answer their prayers.

Give them patience and grace as they wait upon you with expectant yet trusting and patient eyes. Transform them, create in them a new heart, one that loves you more than the temporary relief from their trial.

I pray that the fruit of this trial becomes so great, so amazing, that they will praise you for this trial. Have them peacefully rest in the wisdom that a loving God will bring them through their fire and will be with them every step of the way.

In precious Jesus' name, I pray.

Amen.

APPLICATION QUESTIONS

Getting to the Heart of It

1. Read Daniel 3. How do the faithful actions of Shadrach, Meshach, and Abednego encourage you?

2. Describe a time now or in the past when you have experienced a fiery trial. Specifically, what got you through?

3. What would you do differently if you had to go through it all again?

4. What lessons did you learn through your trial?

5. Did your faith in God increase or decrease because of your trial? Why do you think that happened?

6. List the fruit (good results, changes, etc.) in your life or your family's lives that would not have happened had you not gone through the trial.

7. Are you able to thank God for your trials? Why or why not?

8. Read and memorize "*Give thanks in all circumstances*; for this is God's will for you in Christ Jesus" (1 Thessalonian 5:18 NIV emphasis mine). How can you thank and praise God for your seasons of suffering?

Now to *him who is able to do immeasurably more than all we ask or imagine, according to his power that is at work within us*, to him be glory in the church and in Christ Jesus throughout all generations, for ever and ever! Amen.

~ Ephesians 3:20–21 NIV *emphasis mine*

1. Before presenting your prayer requests to God, remind yourself of whom you are praying to. List five different attributes of God (ones you haven't listed before).

   1 ______________________________
   2 ______________________________
   3 ______________________________
   4 ______________________________
   5 ______________________________

2. List at least five (different from ones listed in previous chapters) blessings in your life that you are grateful for.

   1 ______________________________
   2 ______________________________
   3 ______________________________
   4 ______________________________
   5 ______________________________

3. List your prayer requests.

4. Write down anything else the Lord is speaking to your heart.

5. Finally, praise God in advance for whatever the outcome.

SECTION II
Reasons for Trials

CHAPTER FOUR

Eyes on God

Now the serpent was more crafty than any of the wild animals the LORD God had made. He said to the woman, "Did God really say, 'You must not eat from any tree in the garden'?" The woman said to the serpent, "We may eat fruit from the trees in the garden, but God did say, 'You must not eat fruit from the tree that is in the middle of the garden, and you must not touch it, or you will die.'" "You will not certainly die," the serpent said to the woman. "For God knows that when you eat from it your eyes will be opened, and you will be like God, knowing good and evil."

When the woman saw that the fruit of the tree was good for food and pleasing to the eye, and also desirable for gaining wisdom, *she took some and ate it.* She also gave some to her husband, *who was with her, and he ate it.* Then the eyes of both of them were opened, and they realized they were naked; so they sewed fig leaves together and made coverings for themselves. Then the man and his wife heard the sound of the LORD God as he was walking in the garden in the cool of the day, and they hid from the LORD God among the trees of the garden.

But the LORD God called to the man, "Where are you?"

He answered, "I heard you in the garden, and I was afraid because I was naked; so I hid." And he said, "Who told you that you were naked? Have you eaten from the tree that I commanded you not to eat from?"

~ GENESIS 3:1–11 NIV *emphasis mine*

"DON'T EAT IT." The voice spoke to my heart.

I frowned, holding open the refrigerator door. I looked at it again, turning it over and over in my hand. It was just cheese—herb-crusted soft French chèvre (or goat cheese, to be exact). It was still safely encased in its clear packaging. It was cool to the touch from being in the refrigerator.

"*You know it will make you sick.*" The still, small voice continued.

"How could something I used to eat all the time suddenly make me so sick?" I muttered. Cheese was always my go-to protein choice. It went on and into just about everything I made. Apparently now my body was rejecting it. I could no longer digest the lactose; at least that's what my doctor said.

"Maybe this time it won't," I argued.

The voice was silent.

Frustrated, I grabbed all the makings of the rest of my salad and tossed them on the counter. In between washing the peppery arugula and slicing the sweet grape tomatoes in half, I glanced at the cheese staring back me. It had no idea such a strong debate was ensuing over itself.

The aroma from the cayenne-and-cinnamon-coated walnuts toasting in the oven brought me back to reality. I carefully retrieved them from the steaming cookie sheet. After they cooled, I painstakingly topped my salad with them and the dried cherries.

Still scowling at the cheese, I sprinkled balsamic vinegar and extra virgin olive oil over the green leafy explosion on my plate. My salad was complete—except for the goat cheese, that is.

"The salad is actually crying for it," my mind justified.

I sighed. The voice was right. I would get sick if I ate it. But I also knew how much I loved goat cheese, especially on my salads.

The voice remained silent. It was a test.

I shifted my weight from one leg to the other. I glared at the cheese, debating if the risk was worth it. Minutes went by.

Then, like a guilty child indulging in cookies before dinner, I grabbed the cheese, opened it, and defiantly plopped it on my salad. Maybe if I moved fast, God wouldn't notice.

As I indulged in my masterpiece, the little voice was quiet. Each mouthful exploded with a unique symphony of delicious flavor combinations. My lips pursed in a satisfied smile as I scooped up the last of the dressing-covered walnuts and dried cherries.

An hour later, I was doubled over, clutching my stomach in pain. I felt like I was trying to digest crushed glass. I barely made it to bathroom before I got sick.

Groaning, I slid down on the cold tile floor, blotting the perspiration off my forehead with the frilly "guest-only" hand towel. My skin was clammy, and my stomach still rumbled loudly in protest. I gasped as I grabbed the commode again. "I'm sorry I didn't listen to you, God," I whimpered.

Silence.

I wiped my mouth with the back of my hand.

Finally, when I was able to stand (just barely), I glanced in the mirror. My heart sank. I had dark circles under my eyes, mascara had run down my cheeks, and my skin was ash white with a lovely green tint. Shoulders slumped, I mumbled in repentance, "You have the best for me. I'm sorry for not trusting you, God."

After crawling onto the couch in the fetal position, I prayed for the sickness to subside. I lay there under the blankets until sleep mercifully came.

How often do we do that? Why do we purposely choose things that are wrong or hurtful to ourselves or others? At least for me and the cheese saga, I selfishly and pridefully wanted my own needs to be met regardless of the consequences.

I wonder if Eve felt that same swell of pride as she examined the forbidden fruit in her hand as I did with the goat cheese? Did she experience that same surge of self-sufficiency like I did, right before she indulged? Was she so self-absorbed that she took for granted God's merciful love and protection as I know I've done so many times in the past?

I wonder, in the cool evening wind of that day, what God thought when he walked in his garden. After all, he is omniscient—all-knowing. He knew his children had disobeyed his commands. I'm sure he saw Satan cunningly engage Eve and heard the entire interaction. Did God grieve as he witnessed his daughter so easily believe the serpent's twisting of God's words? I wonder, did God groan when Adam, the appointed leader and protector of his wife, idly stand by as his wife chatted with the enemy?

Was God's heart pierced when Eve took that first bite from the fruit of the forbidden tree of knowledge of good and evil? Did a tear slide down God's cheek when she gave some of the fruit to her husband and he ate it? Did God's heart sink when Adam and Eve first heard the peals of thunder from his approach of condemnation and tried to hide from him, for "conscience makes cowards"?[1] When their bodies "ceased to be the pure abode of a spirit in fellowship with God"[2] and they fumbled to make underwear from fig leaves in a feeble attempt to cover their newfound nakedness, did he sigh and shake his head?

> But God …
>
> ~ Genesis 3:8

But God (my two favorite words in the Bible), in his infinite mercy, *sought them out* (Genesis 3:8–9). How comforting that, despite our sin, God doesn't turn away from us. Instead he lovingly pursues us to give us the chance to repent. And even more so, as we might weigh in as struggling parents, to see that even the children of a perfect and holy God, the ones that he created with his own hands, knowingly rebelled and disobeyed him. So those of us who wonder how our children aren't flawless despite our efforts, look to God for comfort. He faced the same struggles with Adam and Eve.

What was God's response to their trespasses against him? He called Adam to account for the sins committed in the garden (Genesis 3:9–11). Unfortunately, Adam's response was less than admirable. Repentance (admitting and turning from sin to God) was far from their hearts. Adam blamed God: "The woman you put here with me—she gave me some fruit from the tree" (Genesis 3:12). Eve persisted with the blame shifting (it's amazing how contagious sin is): "the serpent deceived me" (Genesis 3:13).

Satan didn't *make* either of them sin. But he *did* twist the words of God and he *did* deceive them. Adam and Eve chose to doubt God's goodness. *They* put the fruit in their mouth. *They* swallowed sin for all humanity. *They* made a bad choice. *They* listened to the enemy instead of God. *They* took their eyes off God.

The one thing I found interesting in this interaction is the enemy's strategy. He manipulated one of them—in this case, the more emotional half—to distrust God. In doing so, he brought sin and death into the world.

Satan didn't *make* either of them sin.... *They* took their eyes off God.

Even today, with half of all marriages ending in divorce, Satan is at work placing a sliver of doubt, discontentment, anger, lies, unbelief, and thoughts of sexual sin into the hearts and minds of husbands and wives. In doing so, divorce becomes commonplace.

Having experienced firsthand the rippling pain from divorce on both sides—both as a victim (an adult child of divorce) and as a participant (my first marriage ended in divorce)—I firmly believe a stable, God-honoring marriage is so important. I can see why Satan wants so desperately to destroy this covenant: the marital union reflects Christ's relationship with the church, and in divorce, sin and brokenness are multiplied throughout our society. The guilt and pain from a divorce create an unwarranted divide between us and God. I believe that's Satan's end game: unravel humanity through sin by pulling us farther from a loving God.

This doesn't mean if you've walked through a divorce or are a child of divorce, you're tainted and unable to receive God's grace, blessing, and salvation. We all have sinned and fallen short of the glory of God (Romans 3:23), and there is not one righteous, not one (Romans 3:10). We *all* need Jesus to cover us with his blood so that all our sins are forgiven, including the pain and sin from a divorce.

We *all* need Jesus to cover us with his blood so that all our sins are forgiven.

Back to the garden. The next step in good parenting is to establish consequences. God cursed the serpent above all animals, commanded him to slither around on his belly and to eat dust all the days of his life (Genesis 3:14). How humbling! The diet of Lucifer, the glorious "light-bearer" or "shining one"[3] has been reduced to one of a dust mite—he now must eat the dust that flakes off man. No wonder he's so angry with us!

God then cursed Eve and all women with multiplied pain during childbirth (one physician once told me that there is no anatomical reason why women have such pain during childbirth except from the curse). God also gave women the desire to control their husbands and placed their husbands to rule over them (Genesis 3:16 NLT).

Last, God cursed man and the ground, and brought death into the world because Adam listened to his wife (we as wives need to be careful of the counsel we give our husbands) and took his eyes off God (Genesis 3:17–19). God cursed the ground and swore that man "will struggle to scratch a living from it" (Genesis 3:17 NLT). And he declared man will return to the dirt from which he was created, "'for out of it you were taken; for you are dust, and to dust you shall return'" (Genesis 3:19 NLT).

Yet, amid all the affliction, there is a glimmer of hope. God promised a Savior, Jesus Christ, as one who will have the victory over Satan, one who will crush his head, even though Satan will strike his heel (Genesis 3:15 NIV) on the cross. I find it interesting that Satan is equated with a roaring lion prowling around, looking for someone to devour (1 Peter 5:8), although even in the garden, Satan's defeat is declared inevitable. Our final victory has already been won!

Even though our Savior has come and died for our sins, and we are no longer under the curse (Galatians 3:13), we are living in a world between gardens: Eden and heaven. Therefore, we still struggle with sin and repeat Adam's and Eve's fateful actions, just like I did with the cheese. We know what is right and wrong. We know what pleases God. Still, we break God's commands multiple times a day, if not with our actions, then with our thoughts. We are all modern-day Adams and Eves.

> We'll have three surprises in heaven: the people who we thought *would* be there *aren't there*, the people who we thought would *never* be there *are there*, and *we are there*.

Unfortunately, some people self-righteously blame Adam and Eve. One lady said, "The first thing I'm going do when I get to heaven is slap Eve." I'm sure once she's there, she'll be so awed by the mountain of *her* sin that was paid for by Jesus on the cross that she won't even bother to condemn and strike Eve. That is if Eve is even there. Someone once told me we'll have three surprises in heaven: the people who we thought *would* be there *aren't there*, the people who we thought would *never* be there *are there*, and *we are there*.

If we really search our own heart, we know if Adam and Eve didn't make that ominous decision, we would have. We would have failed the exam. We would have doubted God. We would have taken that irrevocable step outside God's boundaries that he had so generously drawn in pleasant places (Psalm 16:6).

We also would have nodded our heads in agreement with Satan as he twisted God's words. We would have distrusted our Creator. We would have taken that perilous bite out of the forbidden fruit. We also would have wanted to be like God, with our eyes opened to good and evil (Genesis 3:5). Then we would have realized that we are naked and in desperate need of covering from a Savior. We would have been the ones who caused the Fall and were forced to leave the garden.

Once, as I was praying, the Lord spoke to my heart, "All of humanity's sin, including the first sin, starts from one singular sin: the sin of *unbelief that* God is not good." Every sin is based on the false assumption that God is not good—that he will not provide good gifts in his perfect timing, that he will not take care of us, that the death of his Son is not enough to take away our sins, and that we still need to somehow earn our righteousness (which is impossible) to gain access to God.

> "All of humanity's sin, including the first sin, starts from one singular sin: the sin of unbelief that God is not good."
>
> ~ God

Living in a fallen world, we are sporadically hamstrung by afflictions from that bite of the forbidden fruit. We experience pain from the shrapnel of other people's sins. Unfortunately, this is the product of life outside of the garden after the Fall. Before the Fall, we had sweet communion with God. Can you even imagine being Adam and Eve before the Fall? They were face-to-face with God in the garden. Everything they needed was provided for them. They were surrounded by such intense beauty, with only minimal yet joyful work.

They walked with God. They shed no tears. They felt no agony, no suffering, no betrayal, no frustrations, no sickness, and no death. They were at peace with God. They had no need to grow or become better through trials. The end goal was already met. Their only assignment was to expand the borders of the garden of Eden. But all that was before the Fall.

Now things are different. Today, God uses trials to bring us closer to him. They are a time of testing, just like he vetted Adam and Eve. Like a pot boiling over under intense heat, trials bring out what's inside each one of us. They reveal what we hide behind our everything-is-fine mask.

Trials puncture the paper-thin protective barrier surrounding our hearts. They expose our fears, anger, bitterness, and unforgiveness. They multiply the lies of unbelief that God is not good. God uses our afflictions to remove these falsehoods and idols from our hearts. One of the most effective ways these not-so-welcomed "little gods" can be extracted is by God's delicate yet exceedingly sharp redemptive scalpel through a trial.

Since God intimately knows our hearts, he mercifully uses our suffering to reveal our sin and our desperate need for a Savior. He skillfully eradicates the things that block us from complete worship and sweet communion with him. As we turn to him, he fills our God-sized hole from our deep wounds of the past. The greater the intensity and the more gaping the abyss, the more God fills us up. Nothing else in this world can pacify us.

Since God intimately knows our hearts, he mercifully uses our suffering to reveal our sin and our desperate need for a Savior.

I wonder, if Adam's and Eve's focus had been only on God, would they have even heard the enemy? Imagine how differently that day and the rest of our lives might have gone. I wonder the same for you and me. If we lifted our gaze to God today and looked solely to him, how differently would our day go? Would our unbelief completely vaporize?

As we all know, times of suffering can be excruciating. During a time when I was spiritually suffocating in deep waters, I would force myself to go out for long walks. It gave me time to pray and seek God. He would offer me manna—sweet words of comfort that drizzled down over me. They completely altered my reality and allowed me to breathe again.

One day as I happily tucked my toddler in the stroller and fastened the leash on to our territorial family dog's collar, the Lord spoke to me. On the way home, we saw this beautiful yellow retriever and her owner. They were calmly standing outside; the yellow lab had her back to us. Her master was facing us but not looking at us. Our eight-pound fluffy white attack dog ferociously defended her ground as she barked herself into a frenzy, wrapping her bright red leash around the stroller, almost strangling my little one.

> If we lifted our gaze to God today and look solely to him, how differently would our day go?

As I was trying to save my child's life by untying the savage puff ball, I was in awe of the peaceful dog and its owner. The dog's master was solely fixated on his dog. And the dog's attention was completely locked on her master, ignoring the obnoxiously barking cotton ball. God, as he had before, amid all the chaos, spoke…

Eyes on God

Do you see that? Do you see where the focus of that dog's attention lies? Does it lie in the barking, snarling, and growling of an untamed beast? Or does its attention, despite the barrage of insults and the temporary annoyance, remain completely transfixed on her master?

Do you see the beauty in being single-focused? Do you see the peace that emulates from that dog who is transfixed not on the voice of the enemy, but on the face of her master?

That is exactly what I want you to do.

That is what I am using this trial for in your life. I am using this trial to train you. To train your focus to always be on me, despite the angry barking of the enemy no matter how loud, hateful, or hurtful he is.

You need only to look to me. Be transfixed on me. Be so immersed in my Word, my majesty, my commands, my glory, my statues, that the hissing of the enemy will not even permeate your ears, thoughts, or mind. So that despite the trial, deep waters, season of suffering, or difficult circumstance, your focus is always on me.

Your thoughts should *not* be on your discomfort, pain, or agony. Nor should it reside on the sins of others as they angrily bark at you like an untamed beast. Your attention needs to remain on me, your God, your Kinsman Redeemer, and your Savior, despite your environment.

You need to *lift your gaze to me*. For I AM your God, your source of sustenance, power, and strength. For when you are *weak*, I am *strong*; my grace is sufficient for you. I will never cast you aside.

I AM your God. *Lift your gaze to me* despite your trials. For I uphold you in the middle of your deep waters, my child.

My will always prevails.

Lift your gaze to me, your God.

During times of suffering, that ever-so-slight tilt in your vision toward God, especially amid the vicious barking of the enemy, can be challenging. It is a physical *and* spiritual act of obedience. Even with prayer, we still need to train ourselves to focus on God and praise him despite our circumstances:

> May my accusers be put to shame and consumed; with scorn and disgrace may they be covered who seek my hurt. *But I will hope continually and will praise you yet more and more.* (Psalm 71:13–14 emphasis mine)

My prayer for you is that your God who so delicately knit you together in your mother's womb would draw near to you and comfort you. I pray that you would first and foremost behold your God. I also pray you would not waver, and your gaze would be captivated and lifted to your God as I pray over you ...

Dear God,

Please draw near my friends as they are reading this. Help them lift their gaze to you. It's only by your grace they can remain transfixed on your face as the enemy assails them with lies, deceit, and anger. Pour out your love upon them.

Help them completely lock in on you, your face, the great Alpha and Omega, and the Great I AM. Imbed the time-tested promises of your Word on their heart. As they are transfixed by you, silence the enemy's lies. Let the words of the accuser fall on deaf ears.

Bless them with your peace that surpasses all understanding. Fill them with your presence, your Holy Spirit. Impart on them your words of promise and hope. Stir in them a spirit of worship of their one true God who is on the throne. For you are their God, the one who will never reject them.

Bless them, oh God. Let your praise be forever on their lips. Give them joy that only comes from you. Show up *big* in their lives, even just for a moment of comfort.

Give them a confirmation in the flesh that you, the Great I AM, are still on the throne, you have *not* forgotten about them, you hear their cries, and they are treasured by you, most high God.

Move mightily in their lives. Help them focus on you as you are preparing them for something greater. Enable them to persevere in a way that glorifies you, oh Lord.

Give them your peace so that daily worship is part of their very being.

In Jesus' precious name.

Amen!

APPLICATION QUESTIONS

Getting to the Heart of It

The Fall is the primary reason we experience trials, suffering, and even death. We daily experience the consequences of their sin. Please note, your responses to the questions in this chapter or any other chapter might be too personal to share in a group. If you don't feel comfortable sharing, then don't. As always, use discernment and discretion when sharing your heart in a group setting.

1. Read Genesis 3 aloud.

2. Why do you think God even put the tree of the knowledge of good and evil in the garden of Eden?

3. Do you think it was a test? Why or why not?

4. Do you think you would have made a different choice than Adam and Eve did? Why or why not?

5. Was there ever a time when you were tempted to do or say something you knew was wrong and you did it anyway (like me and the cheese)? Describe.

6. What were the consequences of your actions?

7. Were they as severe as Adam and Eve's consequences? Why do you think so?

8. What lessons did you learn from your time of testing?

9. In hindsight, would you repeat your response if faced with the same situation? Why or why not?

10. How are you being tested and lured away from focusing on God by the bait of unbelief by our enemy?

11. What helps you *lift your gaze* to your God and completely disregard the voice of your enemy?

Prayer Journal

Set your minds on things above, not on earthly things.

~ Colossians 3:2 NIV

1. Before presenting your prayer requests to God, remind yourself of who you are praying to. List five different attributes of God you haven't listed yet:

   1 ______________________________
   2 ______________________________
   3 ______________________________
   4 ______________________________
   5 ______________________________

2. List at least five blessings (different ones from previous chapters) in your life you are grateful for:

   1 ______________________________
   2 ______________________________
   3 ______________________________
   4 ______________________________
   5 ______________________________

3. List your prayer requests:

   ____
   ____
   ____

4. Write down anything else the Lord is speaking to your heart…

5. Finally, praise God in advance for whatever the outcome.

CHAPTER FIVE

Do You Trust Me?

> [Job] possessed 7,000 sheep, 3,000 camels, 500 yoke of oxen, and 500 female donkeys, and very many servants, so that this man was the greatest of all the people of the east. Now there was a day when the sons of God came to present themselves before the LORD, and Satan also came among them. The LORD said to Satan, "From where have you come?" Satan answered the LORD and said, "From going to and fro on the earth, and from walking up and down on it." And the LORD said to Satan, *"Have you considered my servant Job, that there is none like him on the earth, a blameless and upright man, who fears God and turns away from evil?"*
>
> Then Satan answered the LORD and said, "Does Job fear God for no reason? Have you not put a hedge around him and his house and all that he has, on every side? You have blessed the work of his hands, and his possessions have increased in the land. But stretch out your hand and touch all that he has, and he will curse you to your face." And the LORD said to Satan, *"Behold, all that he has is in your hand. Only against him do not stretch out your hand."*
>
> So Satan went out from the presence of the LORD.
>
> ~ JOB 1:3, 6–12 *emphasis mine*

EVERYTHING SEEMED TO stop and focus on me. It was as if I were a black hole. My stomach shriveled up into a little ball.

The cashier popped her gum impatiently.

Embarrassed, I handed her another credit card. It didn't work either.

"You know, we take cash," she flatly stated as she handed the card back to me.

I wanted to crawl into a cave and die. Forcing a smile, I gave her my fifth credit card. My seven-month-old baby started to wail in her baby seat. I sighed, looking from her to the cart full of diapers, wipes, and baby food.

"Again, we take cash," the cashier repeated, this time with piercing distain as she gave the last card back.

The customers behind me angrily pushed their carts to another line.

I bit my lip to hold back the tears. Mortified, I handed her the last few twenties in my wallet.

She ripped them from my hand with another loud pop of her gum.

The air in the store smelled stale, and I unzipped my jacket. It was suddenly unusually hot in here. My little one started to howl.

The cashier dismissed me with a snarl, my receipt, and a few coins.

Red-faced, I quickly pushed my cart with my crying child out of the store. Tears ran down my cheeks as I loaded my baby and bags into my luxury SUV.

After a deep breath, I forced a smile and a giggle for my little one. I filled her chubby little hand with a large rectangular-shaped teething biscuit from the box I just purchased. She shrieked in delight and tried unsuccessfully to shove the whole thing sideways into her mouth. Undeterred, she sucked on the corner with large saucer-shaped eyes, stopping periodically to squeal with joy.

I got in the car and dialed the bank and credit card companies. A nice lady with a pleasant voice informed me I had been removed from all joint marital accounts. I politely thanked her and hung up, then laid my head on the steering wheel and wept. I had known this would happen. But more warning than finding out in the checkout line of a baby store that I was broke, would have been nice.

It's a sad day when you realize you're financially devastated. It's even more bleak when you know in your heart things are going to get much worse.

I wonder if Job felt that way too. I don't think he realized when he lost all his children and his wealth that it was going to get even worse, and that he was the pawn in a wager between God and Satan.

I've often thought of that interaction. Can you even envision it? I mean really? God and Satan even in the same heavenly realm? Wouldn't the holiness of God just incinerate Satan? I mean, *poof*! No ashes. No soot. Satan, our opposer, would be completely oxidized. Wouldn't that be lovely? No enemy to tempt us. No adversary to afflict us. No spiritual warfare. But then ... we would have no need for a Savior.

One thing I find interesting is when *all* the sons of God or messengers (their names are descriptive of their duties)[1] come to present themselves before the Lord, our accuser, Satan, was included in that lot. Just think of it: our LORD God, Elohim-Jehovah,[2] *allowed* Satan, whose job is to oppose men in their standing before God,[3] to even come into his presence.

It was here that our enemy receives his marching orders and permission to execute them. This act of capitulation as our opposer taunted Providence[4] makes me ponder Satan's power—or lack thereof. He is subject and submissive to God's sovereignty and authority. Our enemy is just a fallen angel (Isaiah 14:12–15 NKJV) with limited and finite powers. And when it was his turn to check in with the Creator of the universe, the only Supreme Being,[5] God asked Satan if he has considered his faithful servant Job.

Now Job was one of the wealthiest and most respected men on the planet. His net worth *just* in camels was half the wealth of a modern-day Persian king.[6] He had additional sources of wealth from his immense crops, assembly of servants, and other riches. He was also blessed with seven sons and three daughters. Job would daily rise early and make continual sacrifices for himself and his children. He even offered sacrifices for his family in case they sinned unintentionally. Job was a righteous man and was respected by his peers at the city gate. Most importantly, God, who knows each of our hearts, declared Job "blameless and upright" (Job 1:1–2).

After God finished bragging on Job, Satan retorted that Job is faithful and loves God *only* because of Job's cushy life. Satan asserted that Job's faith was weak and that he would buckle and curse God with a little heat from Satan's blowtorch. God permitted Satan to use evil against his servant with one condition: Satan was not to harm Job's health. God *lifted* the hem of Job's protection and *allowed* Satan to afflict him.

The winds cataclysmically changed in Job's life. One day he was blessed; the next day he was cursed. All of Job's ten children perished in a freak accident. His multitude of oxen and herds of camels were slaughtered by violent savages. Every one of his vast crops, sheep, and servants were incinerated from fire from heaven (Job 1:14–19). He was now financially devastated, childless, had no servants, and had lost all his retirement (flocks and herds). Job was mercifully left with his health and his wife. And what was Job's response? Worship:

> Naked I came from my mother's womb, and naked shall I return. The LORD gave, and the LORD has taken away; blessed be the name of the LORD. (Job 1:20–21)

Wow. I'm not sure I could have even formed that thought, let alone spoke it.

Job still adored God, even when his life was completely pulverized. Unbeknownst to Job, there was another God-assembly and all the sons of God were to once again present themselves to God. Satan still had his sights on Job, despite Job's unlikely response of worship amid such suffering.

When Satan came again to pay to homage to God, God asked him:

> "Have you considered my servant Job, that there is none like him on the earth, a blameless and upright man, who fears God and turns away from evil? He still holds fast his integrity, although you incited me against him to destroy him without reason." Then Satan answered the LORD and said, "Skin for skin! All that a man has he will give for his life." And the LORD said to Satan, "Behold, he is in your hand; only spare his life." (Job 2:3–4, 6)

Sadly, Satan now had access to Job's health; the results were not pretty. He splattered the once-rich patriarch who was now penniless and childless with painful sores all over his body. Job was now oozing from the soles of his feet to the top of his head. What was Job's response? Once again, his reaction challenges me. Sitting in ashes, he picked up a piece of broken pottery and started to gently scrape off his sores (Job 2:7–8).

Job still has his wife, but she wasn't much of an asset. After the second round of God-authorized affliction, she counseled her husband to curse God and die. She's not someone I want with me in the trenches! I want someone who encourages me to lift my gaze to God. God-cheerleaders are essential while we're being refined like silver in the fiery crucible of a trial.

To add insult to injury (literally), Job's three friends, accompanied by their younger protégé, arrived. They had come to comfort Job in his affliction. Job's physical condition was so severe that they didn't even recognize him. They sat with him for seven days in supportive silence. They uttered an occasional sympathetic wail or a sorrowful cry. Then they spoke. That's when the trouble started. They applied their flawed theology to Job: only sinners are afflicted with calamity, the innocent always prospers (Job 4), and Job obviously has some hidden sin he hasn't confessed and needs to repent (Job 8). And they added that Job deserves worse than the suffering he has received (Job 11).

> God-cheerleaders are essential while we're being refined like silver in the fiery crucible of a trial.

We all have received this type of counsel from those closest to us. As we walk through a life-shattering trial, it seems we are always looking for a scapegoat. But if God is sovereign and allowed this calamity to come upon Job, then is God to blame for our sufferings?

If we place the responsibility for our trials on God, are we therefore putting ourselves above God? Are we by our very thoughts and deeds declaring ourselves to be wiser than God? Maybe we believe God was asleep at the wheel of the universe when this tragedy transpired? Or perhaps God was distracted for a moment and missed this pummeling we are receiving from the enemy?

In God's infinite wisdom, he authorized this season of testing for Job. Thankfully, God clearly saw his servant Job's heart, just like he sees ours. And God knows the outcome. The war is already won. For those of us trying to keep our head above the water line in the deep waters of our trial, that can be a hard truth to swallow.

How comforting is it for us to know that if God allows hardships, then he will use them as a redemptive tool to make us more like Christ. As we see in Job, Satan can and will use our environment, possessions, children, health, and the vanity of material objects to steal our affections from God. It is his goal to shift our gaze from God to our hopeless situation. By God's grace in the proper adjustment of our vision, Satan's feeble efforts to steal our joy during our trials dissolve. God uses Satan's trifling attempts to steal our joy to draw us closer to the only true source of comfort—our Creator.

God's plans for us cannot be thwarted. Period. He is in control of everything in our lives. If God uses *all* things for good for those who love him and are called to his purposes (Romans 8:28 NKJV), then God can use even the enemy's evil schemes and our sin for his glory and our good. That's how big he is!

How comforting is it for us to know that if God allows hardships, then he will use them as a redemptive tool to make us more like Christ.

The Bible clearly unveils God's attributes. God is omnipresent—he is always present. He is omniscient—all-knowing. He is omnipotent—all-powerful, there is no other authority above him. He is transcendent—he is without time constraints.

So many of these attributes are clearly revealed in the last chapters of Job. Job protested that his season of suffering is unjust. He defiantly demanded answers from God for the reason for his suffering (Job 12). And he even went so far as to proclaim that it would have been better if he was never born (Job 3:1–3, 10:18).

> God's plans for us cannot be thwarted. Period.

Heat from trials can do that to all of us. It makes us forget that our God is good. We fail to remember how much God loves us. We forget that God uses all things for good, even evil, sickness, destruction, and death.

God in his infinite mercy and wisdom didn't answer Job's complaints directly. Instead, in the middle of an F5 tornado, God cited the creation of the world:

> Then the LORD answered Job out of the whirlwind and said: "Who is this that darkens counsel by words without knowledge? Dress for action like a man; I will question you, and you make it known to me. Where were you when I laid the foundation of the earth? Tell me, if you have understanding. Who determined its measurements—surely you know! Or who stretched the line upon it? On what were its bases sunk, or who laid its cornerstone, when the morning stars sang together and all the sons of God shouted for joy? Or who shut in the sea with doors when it burst out from the womb, when I made clouds its garment and thick darkness its swaddling band, and prescribed limits for it and set bars and doors, and said, 'Thus far shall you come, and no farther, and here shall your proud waves be stayed'? Have you commanded the morning since your days began, and caused the dawn to know its place, that it might take hold of the skirts of the earth, and the wicked be shaken out of it? It is changed like clay under the seal, and its features stand out like a garment. From the

wicked their light is withheld, and their uplifted arm is broken. Have you entered into the springs of the sea, or walked in the recesses of the deep? Have the gates of death been revealed to you, or have you seen the gates of deep darkness? Have you comprehended the expanse of the earth? Declare, if you know all this. Where is the way to the dwelling of light, and where is the place of darkness, that you may take it to its territory and that you may discern the paths to its home? You know, for you were born then, and the number of your days is great! Have you entered the storehouses of the snow, or have you seen the storehouses of the hail, which I have reserved for the time of trouble, for the day of battle and war? What is the way to the place where the light is distributed, or where the east wind is scattered upon the earth? Who has cleft a channel for the torrents of rain and a way for the thunderbolt, to bring rain on a land where no man is, on the desert in which there is no man, to satisfy the waste and desolate land, and to make the ground sprout with grass? Has the rain a father, or who has begotten the drops of dew? From whose womb did the ice come forth, and who has given birth to the frost of heaven? The waters become hard like stone, and the face of the deep is frozen. Can you bind the chains of the Pleiades or loose the cords of Orion? Can you lead forth the Mazzaroth in their season, or can you guide the Bear with its children? Do you know the ordinances of the heavens? Can you establish their rule on the earth? Can you lift up your voice to the

> clouds, that a flood of waters may cover you? Can you send forth lightnings, that they may go and say to you, 'Here we are'? Who has put wisdom in the inward parts or given understanding to the mind? Who can number the clouds by wisdom? Or who can tilt the waterskins of the heavens, when the dust runs into a mass and the clods stick fast together?" (Job 38:1–38)

I don't think we will ever fully understand how awesome God is until we see him face-to-face at our judgment. In the verses above, God displayed his knowledge of all living things in the world. He demonstrated intimate awareness of each one of their needs before even they knew them. He'd already providentially met each one. Then God challenged Job, "Shall a faultfinder contend with the Almighty? He who argues with God, let him answer it" (Job 40:2).

Job humbly responded that he had no idea what he was even talking about in questioning a holy, perfect, all-powerful, almighty God. He covered his mouth and stated that he can speak no more to the one who has created everything that Job can see, touch, breathe, and feel (Job 40:4–5). In God's infinite mercy, he challenged Job. God unveiled that Job condemned God with the same hand without knowledge, as Job's three friends did to Job. They knew not what they spoke of:

> Then the LORD answered Job out of the whirlwind and said: "*Dress for action like a man; I will question you, and you make it known to me.* Will you even put me in the wrong? Will you condemn me that you may be in the right? Have you an arm like God, and can you thunder with a voice like his?

Adorn yourself with majesty and dignity; clothe yourself with glory and splendor. Pour out the overflowings of your anger, and look on everyone who is proud and abase him. Look on everyone who is proud and bring him low and tread down the wicked where they stand. Hide them all in the dust together; bind their faces in the world below. Then will I also acknowledge to you that your own right hand can save you.

Behold, Behemoth, which I made as I made you; he eats grass like an ox. Behold, his strength in his loins, and his power in the muscles of his belly. He makes his tail stiff like a cedar; the sinews of his thighs are knit together. His bones are tubes of bronze, his limbs like bars of iron.

He is the first of the works of God; let him who made him bring near his sword! For the mountains yield food for him where all the wild beasts play. Under the lotus plants he lies, in the shelter of the reeds and in the marsh. For his shade the lotus trees cover him; the willows of the brook surround him. Behold, if the river is turbulent he is not frightened; he is confident though Jordan rushes against his mouth. Can one take him by his eyes, or pierce his nose with a snare?"

Can you draw out Leviathan with a fishhook or press down his tongue with a cord? Can you put a rope in his nose or pierce his jaw with a hook? Will he make many pleas to you? Will he speak to you soft words? Will he make a covenant with you to take him for your servant forever? Will you play with him as with a bird, or will you put him on a leash for your girls? Will traders bargain over him? Will they divide him up among the merchants? Can you fill his skin with harpoons or his head with fishing spears? Lay your hands on him; remember the battle—you will not do it again!

Behold, the hope of a man is false; he is laid low even at the sight of him. No one is so fierce that he dares to stir him up.

Who then is he who can stand before me? Who has first given to me, that I should repay him? Whatever is under the whole heaven is mine.

I will not keep silence concerning his limbs, or his mighty strength, or his goodly frame. Who can strip off his outer garment? Who would come near him with a bridle? Who can open the doors of his face? Around his teeth is terror. His back is made of rows of shields, shut up closely as with a seal. One is so near to another that no air can come between them. They are joined one to another; they clasp each other and cannot be separated.

His sneezings flash forth light, and his eyes are like the eyelids of the dawn. Out of his mouth go flaming torches; sparks of fire leap forth. Out of his nostrils comes forth smoke, as from a boiling pot and burning rushes. His breath kindles coals, and a flame comes forth from his mouth. In his neck abides strength, and terror dances before him. The folds of his flesh stick together, firmly cast on him and immovable. His heart is hard as a stone, hard as the lower millstone.

> When he raises himself up the mighty are afraid; at the crashing they are beside themselves. Though the sword reaches him, it does not avail, nor the spear, the dart, or the javelin. He counts iron as straw, and bronze as rotten wood. The arrow cannot make him flee; for him sling stones are turned to stubble. Clubs are counted as stubble; he laughs at the rattle of javelins. His underparts are like sharp potsherds; he spreads himself like a threshing sledge on the mire. He makes the deep boil like a pot; he makes the sea like a pot of ointment. Behind him he leaves a shining wake; one would think the deep to be white-haired. On earth there is not his like, a creature without fear.
>
> *He sees everything that is high; he is king over all the sons of pride.*" (Job 40:6–24, 41:1–34 emphasis mine)

Job, in deep remorse, humbly and wisely repented of accusing God for not working all things for good, for his unbelief in a holy, almighty, and awesome God, for blaming God for his afflictions, and for only feeling the pain of God's redemptive work. He saw that God allowed this trial not only for Job's good but also for those who might need a reminder of his amazing hand at work during times of suffering. All would be able to see with new eyes how Job walked through his time of testing.

What an amazing transformation of Job's heart. We watched the persecuted Job ride the emotional rollercoaster from worship, to anger, to desiring to have never been born, to finally joyful submission. We ultimately see Job lay down his life, like his Savior, with a willful, all-powerful posture of humility. Only after Job prays for his three wicked comforters does God restore him with ten more children and double the wealth he had from before his time of testing.

It was during my season of suffering that the Lord spoke to my heart, causing me to once again lift my gaze…

Do You Trust Me?

Has not everything, especially every good thing, that I have promised you come to pass? Am I not the God who keeps all his covenant promises with all his chosen vessels? Have I not anointed you, brought you through the fires of purification without one single hair on your head singed? Has not each trial I have brought you through produced so much rich fruit that each time you are amazed?

Are you *not* a child of God? Do I *not* delight in you? Do you *not* have my immeasurable favor upon you? Are you *not* blessed?

Have I *not* reached down with my sovereign hand and plucked you out of many destructive situations where many others would have perished?

Do you *not* trust ME? Put your trust in me, my child, *not* man! I will sustain you.

These difficult events in your life are not coincidental. They are carefully orchestrated for the continual purification and sanctification of your heart. Am I *not* a sovereign, loving God? Am I *not* faithful? Am I *not* trustworthy? Again, do I *not* delight in you?

Put your trust in *me*, my child. Allow yourself to fall and rest into my sovereign, yet *very* capable hands.

I have you, my child. Trust *me*.

Like Job, I doubted God's care, love, and sovereign hand in my life during my darkest moments. I was not trusting that God was working all things out for my greater good, because I couldn't see it at the time.

What the enemy used in my life to attempt to destroy me, God used for good.

What the enemy attempted to use to humiliate me, God used to humble me.

What the enemy used to torment me, God used to cultivate compassion in me for others who are suffering.

What the enemy used to break me, God used to grow my faith.

What lies the enemy fed me—telling me there was no hope—God used to teach me this was just a season and how to *lift my gaze*.

God used the enemy's wicked ways to mold me and teach me to be more submissive to his divine will—just like his Son, Jesus Christ, my Savior, who was obedient even to the point of death. Jesus took my sins upon the cross and died for me so that I never will experience separation from God.

What lies the enemy fed me—telling me there was no hope—God used to teach me this was just a season and how to *lift my gaze*.

By reading Job, especially chapters giving us a glimpse of how amazing God is, it forces us to lift our gaze above our trial and fixate on him. It's then we realize how powerless our enemy is against the authority and power of God.

I'm sure Job's life resonates with many of us on several different levels. Maybe you've also been hit with several rounds of seemingly unbelievable trials at once. Perhaps you have been wounded by friendly fire from well-meaning loved ones. Or possibly you're like me and are shaking your fist at God, telling him that it's not fair, that you've lived a righteous life and don't deserve to suffer. Regardless of your situation, the Lord wants to comfort you, and give you hope, a future (Jeremiah 29:11), and his peace (John 14:27).

God wants you to get to know him better through his Word. He wants to make known to you his irrevocable promise of eternal life through his Son, Jesus Christ. I have no doubt God desires to wrap his arms around you, comfort you with his Holy Spirit, and bless you with his presence. Unbelievably, these things turn out to be more satisfying than the alleviation of the trial.

If you haven't trusted in Jesus Christ as your personal Savior, I implore you to do so. Either way, this is my prayer for you…

Oh Lord,

If any of my friends who are reading this right now are not one of your children and they have not repented from their sins, regardless of what they have done, no matter how heinous, please reach down and touch their hearts.

Help them turn from their waywardness, reverse direction, and have them run to you. You are right there with them just like the loving father in the story of the prodigal son, waiting and watching with open arms for them to turn from their life of perdition and come back to you, their Creator, their Father, their Lord. Oh Lord, have them cry out to you.

Have them ask for your forgiveness.

Allow them to see your mercy, how you freely forgive *all* who sin and fall short of perfection. Reveal to them how your Son's death on the cross was the complete payment for *all* of their sins.

Let them receive the knowledge and comfort that they are forgiven.

Have them *turn*, *repent*, and *trust* in you, Jesus Christ, for their salvation.

Bless them with sweet communion with you, our holy God, for all of eternity.

Oh Lord, touch their heart with your Holy Spirit.

And if they are being refined by fires like Job's—if there is *no* hope in the flesh—use your grace to *lift their gaze* to you, their God who created them and loves them enough to sacrifice your most precious possession, your Son's life in payment for their sins. Have them rest in the knowledge that their sins, which were once as red as scarlet, are now as white as snow, completely washed clean by the blood of their Savior.

Bless them, Father. Increase their love and joy in worshiping you in new ways. Expand their vision of you. Pour out your Spirit into them. Let them, despite their circumstances, have *your* praises on their lips, have their eyes glisten with the deep knowledge of your immense love for them.

Have them know *you*. Have them rejoice in *you*.

Just like a person cannot forget their body, especially when it is pain, you cannot forget your own children when they are in agony and walking through a trial despite the reason for it. Have them know beyond a shadow of a doubt that you are for them. Draw them closer to you, oh God.

Bless them, keep them, and make your face shine down upon them.

Give them *your* peace, oh God.

Let your praises be forever on their lips.

In Jesus' precious name.

Amen!

APPLICATION QUESTIONS

Getting to the Heart of It

1. Have you ever felt forgotten by God? Why or why not? Describe.

2. Have you ever questioned God? Read Job 38–42 aloud.

3. Do you believe even Satan, our enemy, is subject to God's authority? Why or why not? Use Scripture to support your answer.

4. Do you believe Satan's goals are to steal your joy, have you curse God, and have you believe that he is not good? Why or why not?

5. How can you or do you use praying, reading the Bible, and worshiping God as effective tools to thwart the schemes of the enemy?

6. Describe how you pray, read the Bible, and worship God.

> In my distress I called to the LORD; I cried to my God for help. From his temple *he heard my voice; my cry came before him, into his ears.*
>
> ~ PSALM 18:6 NIV *emphasis mine*

1. Before presenting your prayer requests to God, remind yourself of whom you are praying to. List five different attributes of God you haven't listed yet.

   1 ______
   2 ______
   3 ______
   4 ______
   5 ______

2. List at least five additional blessings (that you haven't listed before) in your life that you are grateful for.

   1 ______
   2 ______
   3 ______
   4 ______
   5 ______
   ______

3. List your prayer requests.

4. Write down anything else the Lord is speaking to your heart.

5. Finally, praise God in advance for whatever the outcome.

CHAPTER SIX

The Waters Will Not Overtake You

And [Jonah] said to them, "I am a Hebrew, and I fear the LORD, the God of heaven, who made the sea and the dry land." He said to them, "Pick me up and hurl me into the sea; then the sea will quiet down for you, for *I know it is because of me that this great tempest has come upon you.*" So they picked up Jonah and hurled him into the sea, and the sea ceased from its raging. *Then the men feared the LORD exceedingly, and they offered a sacrifice to the LORD and made vows.*

~ JONAH 1:9, 12, 15–16 *emphasis mine*

THE RAIN PELTED my face as we went up and down the huge waves. I had a death-grip on the edge of the dive boat and looked at the divemaster. His face was calm, but his white-knuckled grasp of his seat betrayed his outward serenity.

"Do you still think this is a good idea?" I screamed over the sound of the engine and the howling wind.

He squinted over at me. "Yes, it will be fine once we're under."

I nodded. My stomach didn't agree; it was doing flip-flops.

The captain, soaking wet, gave us the sign to get ready for our dive. We pulled up our wetsuits, hooked on our tanks, and checked the air pressure as the vessel rocked violently in the storm. Sliding my dive mask down over my face and sticking the regulator in my mouth, I prayed I wouldn't throw up.

We were at the edge of a massive hurricane brewing somewhere in the Caribbean. This band of intense weather was a surprise; it was supposed to shift farther out to sea. Even though the skies were a little ominous when we left the dock, I had no idea it was going to be *this* rough. Hindsight is always 20/20.

Clanging his tank against the side of the boat, the divemaster gave the *okay* sign and fell backward into the raging sea. I watched his head resurface, and he motioned me to join him in the huge waves and rain.

I wavered as a harsh salt-water wave hit me from behind. I felt so insignificant compared to the dark gray sky and angry surf. My heart was beating so fast, and I started to breathe heavy, sucking down all the oxygen in my tank.

The captain desperately held on to the boat's console and screamed over the wind for me to get in. Terrified, I fell backward into the dark ocean as a powerful wave again crashed against me, warning me not to enter.

Amazingly enough, once I was in the water and started to descend, all was quiet. The change in the atmosphere was inexplicable yet disorientating. The peacefulness was soothing as I looked up and saw the boat motoring off to dock somewhere safe while we were enveloped in such calmness. Down below, the florescent aquatic life had no idea of the torrent that ensued on the surface above as they happily swam along, gathering their food from the vibrant coral reefs.

I wonder if Jonah felt terrified as he was thrown overboard in the tempest. How did he respond to the bone-shattering thunder and lightning? Was his sea the same dark shade of indigo as mine? Did the waves in his storm also splatter onto his deck, filling it with water and making it difficult to walk?

In Jonah's situation, his storm was judgment; in mine, it was just plain foolishness. I should never have gone scuba diving in a hurricane. The sailors on my boat were calm, while on Jonah's they were terrified, frantically darting around, screaming to one another. I can't even imagine his chaos. His ship almost capsized and broke apart against the powerful waves as the seaman hurled all their much-needed provisions overboard to salvage the ship and save the passengers.

This cataclysmic event was due to Jonah's defiance of God's directive. Before the storm and even the voyage, God told Jonah to go to Nineveh—the capital of the most barbaric people at that time—and preach repentance. Jonah, not wanting the wicked people of Nineveh to experience the same mercies he as a Hebrew enjoyed, disobeyed God.

He got on a cargo ship traveling over two thousand nautical miles in the opposite direction—as if anyone can run from an all-seeing and all-powerful God. Then when God produced the storm-of-the-millennium in judgment of Jonah's disobedience, as all the sailors were madly praying to their individual gods, Jonah buried himself below deck in one of the dark corners and (of all things) went to sleep. Only after being abruptly awakened by the heathen captain and told to pray to *his* God for help did Jonah finally admit that he was the cause of the tempest.

Then matters got worse for him. As the storm picked up in ferocity, Jonah told everyone he needed to be cast into the sea to satisfy the wrath of God that was upon them (Jonah 1:12). To avoid murder, the sailors desperately tried to row to shore. The forcefulness of the winds and rain increased to oppose their efforts. To save the ship and everyone on board, and praying for God's mercy to be upon them, they hurled Jonah overboard into the churning sea like a tribal sacrifice. As soon as Jonah touched the water, the rains and wind ceased and the sea turned to glass.

I have often wondered, did Jonah struggle? Or did he calmly descend downward in humble submission? Did he look up and see the cessation of the squall? Was he able to witness the retraction of the terrifying storm clouds, wind, and rain, and see the emergence of soft blue skies? Did Jonah, a learned scholar and prophet, recall this Scripture when he sank down into the deep, dark waters?

> You have put me in the depths of the pit, in the regions dark and deep. Your wrath lies heavy upon me, and you overwhelm me with all your waves. (Psalm 88:6–7)

On the surface, the instant serenity must have had an eerie, supernatural feel to it, except for the newly saved sailors who were now loudly praising and offering sacrifices to the God of heaven and earth. Jonah must have felt utterly alone by God and man as the sea enclosed around him, pulling him into the deep waters of his watery coffin.

Miraculously, God sent a large sea creature to swallow him (Jonah 1:17). Some commentaries suggest that God created a creature for such of a time as this, as early Christian paintings depict a sea dragon, while others prefer the more natural interpretation of a whale or mutant great white shark.[1] Either way, Jonah's disobedience met the merciful YAHWEH, the Great I AM, who graciously allowed Jonah to marinate in the belly of this giant sea creature for three days and three nights (Jonah 1:17). It was here, at Jonah's lowest point as he was covered in slimy stomach juices, that he turned from his sin of self-righteousness and cried out to the Lord:

> "I called out to the LORD, out of my distress, and he answered me; out of the belly of Sheol I cried, and you heard my voice.
>
> For you cast me into the deep, into the heart of the seas, and the flood surrounded me; all your waves and your billows passed over me. …
>
> The waters closed in over me to take my life; the deep surrounded me; weeds were wrapped about my head at the roots of the mountains. I went down to the land whose bars closed upon me forever; yet you brought up my life from the pit, O LORD my God.
>
> When my life was fainting away, I remembered the LORD, and my prayer came to you, into your holy temple. Those who pay regard to vain idols forsake their hope of steadfast love. But I with the voice of thanksgiving will sacrifice to you; what I have vowed I will pay. *Salvation belongs to the LORD!*" (Jonah 2:2–9 emphasis mine)

How kind of God to rescue Jonah in the belly of that sea beast and lead him back to his fold as Jonah turned back to God and worshiped him (Jonah 2:9). After three days in that fish, God had the fish vomit up Jonah onto dry land. Jonah obeyed God, went to Nineveh, and started walking through this massive city, preaching the message God first gave him: "Yet forty days, and Nineveh shall be overthrown!" (Jonah 3:4).

Miraculously, one day later (and it took three days just to walk the entire width of the city, according to Jonah 3:3), *all* the people heard Jonah's message and repented. Everyone, including their livestock, wore sackcloth and fasted from food and water as an expression of their sorrow over their sins.

Since the entire city turned from their sins, God showed mercy and did not destroy it as Jonah prophesied. They heeded the perfect message of God from an imperfect man, Jonah. When we're obedient to God, it's astonishing what God can do through us. God used Jonah, even though he was fallible, to bring the good news of salvation and prevent the utter annihilation of a city with a population of over six hundred thousand and their multitudes of livestock.[2]

Sadly, in response to Nineveh's transformational revival and everything that Jonah experienced, his heart was still angry. He shook his puny fist at God and told him he'd rather die than see God spare Nineveh. He justified his initial disobedience by stating he knew his Lord was a gracious and compassionate God, "abounding in steadfast love" (Jonah 4:2), and that God *would* extend mercy if the city repented. Jonah quickly forgot what he learned in the belly of a fish and was resentful that God bestowed on the Ninevites the same compassion and forgiveness he freely received.

Isn't that just like us? We self-righteously attempt to validate our own sinful actions while we condemn others. We are *all* modern-day Jonahs. We *all* have (at least once) run in the opposite direction of God.

Sometimes, God gives us completely over to our consequences—like he did with Jonah and his tempest—and we too are thrown overboard and are drowning in our own sin. Then graciously, after we have been humbled by our eternal Father's firm chastisement and correction, God gives us the grace to lift our gaze and repent. He then forgives us and washes us clean.

We, like Jonah, want mercy, but we don't extend it to others especially those who sin against us. And then we don't repent. We cite some lame excuse that he or she "deserved it" because of how they treated us. We downplay our actions with justifications like "I'm too busy" to repent. We condone our harsh words with "life is too hectic right now" to apologize. We don't serve or show benevolence or love to those who sin against us.

> We, like Jonah, want mercy, but we don't extend it others, especially those who sin against us.

We also are sometimes the very source of our trials. Remember, *Jonah knew God.* He understood a prophet's duties: to obey God and deliver his messages without question. Jonah was the mail carrier, not the bill collector. Instead, Jonah placed himself above God, and in doing so he exposed himself and everyone else on that cargo vessel to God's wrath. Some of us, like Jonah, also experience dire consequences due to our own actions and even inflict deep wounds on others, causing collateral damage.

Even though most of us know the ten commandments (Deuteronomy 5:7–21), we don't keep them. Unfortunately, if you break one, you've broken them all (James 2:10). How many of us have *ever* placed *anything* before our love of God? How about worshiping *anything* but God (ever watch or been a fan at a professional sports game)? How about using the Lord's name *in vain*? Or loving your fellow neighbor as yourself?

How many of us *truly* rest and *don't* work on the Sabbath or at least one day a week? And who has *always* honored and obeyed our parents (including step-parents and in-laws)? How about *never* hating someone—which is considered murder (1 John 3:15)? Or *never* taking something that wasn't yours (including a pen or sticky notes from work)? How about looking lustfully at someone *other* than your spouse—which Jesus stated is adultery (Matthew 5:28)? Or who has *never* told a white lie? And finally, who has *never been* jealous or desired someone else's blessings or giftings?

These commands are impossible for us to keep perfectly, especially in our fallen, messy world. Only one person, Jesus of Nazareth, kept them all. And he, although innocent, died in our place, receiving the just punishment for our actions.

This sweet message of redemptive hope for all of us who have or who are currently reaping what we have sown is like sweet salve to our souls. It is when we are at the nadir of our suffering that our enemy loves to attack us.

Satan wields condemnation like a sharpened machete, aiming for our hearts. He tells us we are not worthy and slyly reinforces that our sins, mistakes, and unwise actions are greater than God's grace. We have falsely believed what we have done is too heinous for God to forgive. We have not yet laid down our trial at the foot of the cross and lifted our gaze to Jesus Christ.

Our focus remains on our affliction. We are overcome with anxiety and fear. We have forgotten how awesome our God really is. We are therefore living in bondage. The realization that our sins have been completely absorbed by the cross eludes us. We have no understanding that we are redeemed and set free.

A wise person once explained the difference between condemnation and conviction this way: If guilt over your own actions leads you to the cross in repentance, you are being *convicted* by the gentle nudge of the Holy Spirit. He will then melt your heart from one of stone to one of flesh. If you are continually replaying your sins to yourself or others, you are in *condemnation* from the enemy. The enemy is using your guilt as a prison to keep you from the redemptive measures of Jesus Christ's complete work on the cross. In this case, deceitful whispers abound of God's conditional love and that God could never love you after what you have done. *These are all lies.* For our enemy is the father of all lies (John 8:44).

If you're struggling with condemnation from your sins, take courage. We, through faith by grace, are spared from God's wrath. Look to your God. If he can forgive the people of Nineveh for their evil actions, he can forgive you too. Run to him. Permit God to wrap his loving arms around you. As you repent, allow the free-flowing waves of grace, mercy, comfort, and love overtake you.

The enemy is using your guilt as a prison to keep you from the redemptive measures of Jesus Christ's complete work on the cross.

Instead of just punishment, God sent his only Son, Jesus, as a sinless, blameless sacrifice for our sins. In his infinite mercy, God's Son received the punishment due us for our sins. Jesus died in our place. He paid our debt for our sins so we will never have to. We are forgiven by a holy God and can have eternal life with him when we pass from this life into the next. We thank you, Jesus, for your perfect and complete act of obedience: the cross.

If we have repented and trusted in Jesus Christ for our salvation, we are forgiven, saved from eternal damnation, and reconciled with God! We *all* have access to a liberating God who desires a more intimate relationship with us. God wants us to turn only to him. This is sometimes why God allows us to reap what we have sown, so we

> God's grace doesn't merely equal our sins: it exponentially exceeds *all* our sins and the *entire* sins of mankind.

can feel the sting from our sins and won't repeat them. Remember, God is so big that he can and does use our disobedience to save others, just like he used Jonah's sin to save all the sailors on that ship. And God's grace doesn't merely equal our sins: it exponentially exceeds *all* our sins and the *entire* sins of mankind.

The Lord spoke similar words to me as my family and I were boating on Lake Marion in Santee, South Carolina. This massive manmade lake has trees protruding right out of the center of it. Apparently, when the government created Lake Marion in the 1940s, they didn't clear the land beforehand. They flooded a thriving forested 100,000+ acre valley.[3]

These Cypress trees survived their watery graves, and after seventy years are now defiantly protruding out of the water. They billow out in the middle of this vast lake and have even sprouted up in the middle of the 75+ foot-deep channel where boats are supposed to safely navigate. These trees grew in complete insubordination to man's efforts to drown them. Here they are rising above the water line, sprouting healthy green leaves. It was there in the middle of this beautiful lake that God spoke tenderly to my heart…

The Waters Will Not Overtake You

Listen, my child. Hear my words. Speak my words to those who are suffering.

Speak tenderly to their souls. Speak to my children who have been overcome by the waters—the deep, dark waters, the waters the enemy had designed to drown them and completely extinguish their dreams and desires. These children of mine have forgotten the visions I gave them, planted in them. Those images are now swollen and waterlogged with grief and pain. They seem like shafts in the wind that have long since blown away for those who are suffering.

Their desires are now so far from them, so unreachable and unattainable, like a child's wild imagination. They have resigned themselves to the seemingly strong yet feeble chains of despair, accepting their fate like beaten and abused animals.

They might momentarily remember those desires, but then quickly dismiss them like one would brush away an insect at a summer picnic. But those long-forgotten dreams are *my* dreams I planted in them; they are my gifts to them. They are seeds that I, their God, placed in their hearts long ago to give them hope and a future. And the enemy, with his lies of hopelessness and despair, has come upon them like a flood with a seemingly arrogant and swift victory.

They fearfully gasp for air, fighting the currents with their own weakening strength, believing that the battle is lost and the enemy has prevailed.

They have forgotten their God, their Savior. They forgot that I AM still on my throne.

Tell them. Tell them there is nothing farther from the truth. The enemy did *not* win. Nor will he, *ever*. For I AM God. And I will never leave my own.

I AM theirs and they are mine. Tell my children I have never left them.

Remind them I have never forgotten them, despite the waves engulfing them. Those waters that they thought were too strong for them—the waters that overcame them with such a sudden rush, and completely overtook them—were not too much for me, their God who undergirds them. These were the very waters I was using to correct them; to humble them; to forcibly lift their gaze to me, their God, Creator, Father, and Kinsman Redeemer. Tell them; speak gently to them. Again, tell them I never will leave them nor forsake them because of the great price I paid for them. Remind them again lest they forget as they flail amid their trials.

Tell them to *lift their gaze*. Tell them to *repent*. Tell them to *trust in their God!* I paid such a high price for them! I gave up my one and only Son, my pure, blameless Lamb for the complete, not partial, but 100 percent payment for their sins.

Tell them *they are redeemed*! And despite what it looks like in the flesh, the here and now, the Great I AM is with them in their darkest hours!

They are *my* children, and I have redeemed them. What the enemy has meant for harm, *I will use for good!* I will cause them to flourish in their deep waters. I will care for them in their affliction. I will gather them up like an eagle on my pinions, in defiance of the attacks from the enemy. I will wrap my wings around them and protect them during their sufferings and the consequences. I *will* cover them. And although trials will come, I *will* be with them. The transformational consequences from their situations will cause them to grow, and spiritually increase exponentially. This will cause them to sprout and soar upward, away from their affliction—the very thing the enemy attempted to use to drown them.

Tell them it is their joy the enemy wants. Tell them to *lift their gaze* and I *will* provide everything for them. For I, and I alone, *reign!*

Tell them they will not be overcome by the waters from their trials. They will defy the restraints of this world; they will sprout out of the waters and they *will* thrive. All because I AM God. There is nothing in this world that I do not have power over or I am not sovereign over.

There is nothing that I cannot or will not use for the good for my children, my called offspring, my precious possessions. My children *will prevail*! My children *will abound*! My children *will overcome*! My children *will thrive*!

Tell them to *lift their gaze* to me. Tell them to look beyond the clouds of their affliction and to *walk by faith, not by sight*. For I AM with them. For I will never reject them.

Tell them to remember:

"When you pass through the *waters*, I will be with you; and through the *rivers*, they shall not *overwhelm* you; when you walk through *fire* you shall not be *burned*, and *the flame shall not consume you*" (Isaiah 43:2 emphasis mine).

Be steadfast and single-focused on me, your Great I AM. For salvation comes from the Lord.

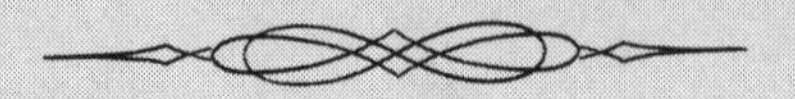

Even though we, like Jonah, might experience a season of suffering, a correction or testing due to our own poor decisions, God is still with us. He doesn't leave us. God doesn't cast us off. He's right there with us, wherever that is—even when we feel like we're drowning in the middle of the tempest, suffocating in the belly of the whale, or self-righteously judging others who have sinned against us.

Your sins, although once like scarlet, are now as white as snow. Your sins are removed from you as far as the east is from the west. By Jesus' completely redemptive work on the cross, you do not need to wear sackcloth and ashes. You are turning to Jesus in repentance for your sins. Remember and hold fast to God's truths over you:

You are forgiven.

You are washed clean.

You are God's.

He paid a great price for you.

You are redeemed.

And this is my prayer for you …

Dear God,

Be with those who are reading this now. Draw close to them. Gather them into your loving arms like only their eternal Father can do. Comfort them. Reveal and dispel the lies of the enemy. Pour out your Holy Spirit into them. Have them confess their sins to you, their loving Father. Remind them that they are redeemed!

Provide confirmation in the flesh that they are loosed from the bondage of their sins! They are forgiven. They are released. There is no sin that is too great for you to cover with your blood. It is finished. You are an extraordinary God.

Where there is sin they are blind to, reveal it to them. Lead them not into condemnation, but to redeeming conviction of their sin. Bring them to your cross. Have them confess their sins and leave them at the foot of your cross. Give them *your* peace, knowing their sins, no matter how atrocious are completely *forgiven*. If they need to make restitution for their actions, provide them boldness, wisdom, discernment, and a clear direction how they should wisely proceed.

Guard them from disobeying your laws. Keep them close to you and immerse them in your Word. Increase your Holy Spirit inside them so they want to do your works not out of obligation but out of their love for their great God and the great price that was paid for them.

Show them how to love again, how to forgive, how to release all bitterness, and how to be a joyful blessing to others. Stir the dreams you placed in their hearts long ago. Ignite that fire you placed in them, a seemingly extinguished flicker of light, which craves your breath to give it the passion, and zeal to blaze again.

Give them a picture of what you have for them once they relinquish their life again to your wise yet gentle reigns. Allow them to focus on that picture of grace when anxiety returns and tempts them in unbelief, taking their thoughts away from you, their God.

Do an amazing, transforming work in their lives. Abundantly bless them even beyond the dreams you have given them. Help them *lift their gaze* beyond their suffering.

Give them the gift of forgiveness. Give them the gift of grace, love, and peace. Fill them with faith. Allow them to look to only you and keep looking to you throughout their season of suffering. Give them your joy. Fixate their eyes solely on your amazing, all-encompassing, life-giving light.

Bless them, my King. Shower them with your glory. Instill in them your power and righteousness. Just as you used Jonah, a disobedient sinner, to save more than six hundred thousand people, use them to lead others to you. Use their sins, shortcomings, and failures to bless and minister to others. Don't waste their tears, trials, or suffering. Use it for their good and your glory, like only a holy, perfect sovereign God can. Bless them, oh King.

Give them your joy during their suffering. Have them reflect your love despite what they are going through. Draw near to them, oh King. Pour your peace into them.

Make your face shine down upon them.

In Jesus' precious name, I pray.

Amen.

APPLICATION QUESTIONS

Getting to the Heart of It

1. Read Romans 8:1 aloud: "There is therefore now no condemnation for those who are in Christ Jesus." Is there anything in your life you still feel guilt over and keep replaying in your mind? If so, list them below.

2. If you're experiencing condemnation from the enemy, write down a complete repentance (accepting, apologizing, and turning from your sins) and an affirmation that you are forgiven. Take those sins to the cross, knowing that they are completely removed from you; all payment has been paid in full by Jesus, and you are no longer enslaved.

3. How does the realization that Jesus Christ received the punishment in full for all your sins—past, present, and future—comfort you?

4. Read aloud and memorize Romans 8:28: "And we know that for those who love God all things work together for good, for those who are called according to his purpose." Pray and ask God to reveal what good has come from your sins.

5. I once heard a pastor say that our sins and the sins others commit against us will be paid for completely on the cross or for eternity in hell. There are no other options. How does that comfort you or concern you? Does that make it easier to forgive those who sin against you?

6. List the dreams, thoughts, and/or passions the Lord has placed on your heart that you have allowed the cares, weight, suffering and trials of this world to eclipse? Journal what your life would look like if these dreams and desires were a reality in your present life and you didn't have any financial or time constraints.

7. Finally, spend time thanking God for your trial and pray he will use it for good.

"*Have faith in God,*" Jesus answered. "Truly I tell you, if anyone says to this mountain, 'Go, throw yourself into the sea,' and does not doubt in their heart but believes that what they say will happen, it will be done for them. Therefore I tell you, *whatever you ask for in prayer, believe that you have received it, and it will be yours.*"

~ MARK 11:22–24 NIV *emphasis mine*

1. Before presenting your prayer requests to God, remind yourself of whom you are praying to. List five different attributes of God you haven't listed yet.

   1 ______________________________
   2 ______________________________
   3 ______________________________
   4 ______________________________
   5 ______________________________

2. List at least five additional blessings (ones you haven't listed before) in your life that you are grateful for.

   1 ______________________________
   2 ______________________________
   3 ______________________________
   4 ______________________________
   5 ______________________________

3. List your prayer requests.

   ____

4. Write down anything else the Lord is speaking to your heart.

5. Finally, praise God in advance for whatever the outcome.

CHAPTER SEVEN

I Know Your Pain

They saw him from afar, and before he came near to them they conspired against him to kill him. "Come now, let us kill him and throw him into one of the pits. Then we will say that a fierce animal has devoured him, and we will see what will become of his dreams." So when Joseph came to his brothers, they stripped him of his robe, the robe of many colors that he wore. And they took him and threw him into a pit. The pit was empty; there was no water in it. Then they sat down to eat. And looking up they saw a caravan of Ishmaelites coming from Gilead, with their camels bearing gum, balm, and myrrh, on their way to carry it down to Egypt. Then Judah said to his brothers, "What profit is it if we kill our brother and conceal his blood? Come, let us sell him to the Ishmaelites, and let not our hand be upon him, for he is our brother, our own flesh." And his brothers listened to him. Then Midianite traders passed by. And they drew Joseph up and lifted him out of the pit, and sold him to the Ishmaelites for twenty shekels of silver. They took Joseph to Egypt.

~ Genesis 37:18, 20, 23–28

"Kim, there's a *serious* problem," said the gruff voice on the phone. "We need to talk."

I held my breath. I recognized the voice and the phone number. Clearing my throat, I croaked out, "Sure, go ahead. What's the problem?"

The voice hesitated. I heard the whining of the high-pitched centrifugal pumps and leaking steam in the background.

"Is everything okay?" I asked in concern.

"Well … no, it's not." Again the voice paused before elaborating.

"Please tell me," I insisted.

I heard him shift his weight to his other leg and move the phone to the other ear. "There's a problem … with that pink stuff that … you put in our closed loops." Each word was measured carefully.

"Okay, yes, the anti-corrosive. What's the problem?" I tightened my fist around the phone. As a chemical sales engineer to some to the most exclusive federal buildings in Washington, D.C., I had run into many competitors who tried to sabotage my work.

"Ah … hmm … Kim, that's the thing," he blurted out. "One of my guys … err … he wasn't looking for it or anything … but he was doing some work down in the nine and ten steam tunnels … and … ah … he saw that the entire waste tank under the floor … was … well … it … was … full and *all pink*!"

"What?!" I yelled into the phone. "Did someone drain one of the closed loops in there?"

"No. They said … you dumped the whole thirty-gallon drum of chemical down the drain tank. That's why it's all pink. We're lucky they didn't drain it so we could see it."

"Are you kidding me?" I spat out. "I spent over twelve hours yesterday down in those hot steam tunnels, rats and all, pumping over ten drums of chemical into those closed loops!"

Silence.

Madly my mind moved at lighting speed. I'd checked all the levels before I left. Everything was fine. This was a serious allegation. I could be terminated, lose my clearance, and possibly be sued.

"Ah, Kim, I know you're new and all . . . and being a subcontractor and all . . . Those drums are heavy . . . and with you having to move them down two flights of those concrete stairs . . . and . . . you just dumped it all down the drain."

"What?" I was pacing now. My integrity was being called into question, and I was starting to seethe. Taking a deep breathe, I exhaled, "Did you check the water in the loops? Is it pink?"

"No. Well, I didn't," he sheepishly responded.

"I'm coming in to check them. In the meantime, get one of the guys to check the water in the loops to confirm its pink." My anger rapidly dropped down to problem-solving as I fired off directives. I continued, "And one more thing. Was anyone working on those loops who could have drained some of the treated water?"

"I don't know. Why?"

"Remember, even if they let out a little bit of treated water in the drain's holding tank, it will turn the whole tank pink if the pH is above 7.0," I calmly explained.

"Oh. I didn't know that."

"Yes, the pink color is only a color additive to make sure the water is alkaline. The nitrates are the chemical that prevents the corrosion, and that's white."

Silence from the other end.

"Look, I'm coming in tomorrow at ten a.m. I'll move around my entire day. I want to get this straightened out." I had never been accused of doing anything illegal, especially dumping chemicals. I was determined to find out what happened and clear my name.

"Okay, Kim. I appreciate that, but I think we got it from here."

"Thanks, but I'm coming in. I'd like to see for myself that everything is fine."

The next day when I went in, I wasn't surprised that the chemical levels were fine and the drainage tank was empty with no pink anywhere to be found. I looked for my contact, but couldn't find him. Finally, one of his guys told me that he was off-site. I asked if he heard anything about the steam tunnels in nine and ten. Without looking at me, he stated that some new guys were working on those pipes yesterday and drained some of the treated water out into the tank, which turned it all pink.

Dumbfounded, I walked away. I could have lost everything for one person's mistake and someone assuming the worst. I was breathing easier now that my name was cleared, but the incident made me more cautious.

Sometimes, wrongs aren't so easily corrected and the trajectory of one's life can be altered dramatically. We see that in the Scripture account of Joseph. He and I were both falsely accused and betrayed. He wasn't vindicated like I was. His ten older brothers were so envious of the favoritism their father showed toward Joseph that they couldn't even speak peacefully to him (Genesis 37:4). They even went so far as to plot to kill him (Genesis 37:18), for the result of unchecked sin is death (Romans 6:23).

Sadly, Joseph and his father, Jacob, were completely oblivious to the hostile fraternal rivalry. Jacob even bestowed on Joseph the honor of the primary son or future leader of his household (ignoring his ten older sons) as he gave him a "richly-embroidered tunic" (Genesis 37:3 ISV). Joseph certainly didn't help the situation when he reported his brothers' shepherding misconduct to their father and openly shared his grandiose dreams of him ruling over *all* of them, including his parents.

When his father sent Joseph to travel seventy-five miles to check on his brothers, neither one of them had any idea of the trial awaiting

Joseph. His older brothers saw Joseph approaching from a far, and they reveled in the opportunity to conspire to kill their unsuspecting teenage brother. Older brother Reuben valiantly intervened and convinced them to throw Joseph into a pit instead, intending to rescue him later.

After stripping him of his coat of many colors, they brutally cast Joseph into a deep, empty pit that was parched from the hot summer months. These pits, or cisterns, were designed to capture rainwater during the rainy season and were narrow at the top with a stone usually rolled over the opening.[1] Joseph would have surely perished from hunger or hypothermia. Then they all happily sat down and ate without any remorse while Joseph screamed for help for hours.

Seeing a caravan of traders headed to Egypt, older brother Judah suggested they sell the favorite son for twenty pieces of silver, the price of a worthless slave. To complete the deception, they dipped the precious symbol of their father's favoritism and love—Joseph's ornate robe that only royalty wore—in goat's blood as physical evidence to their father that their brother had been devoured by a wild beast (Genesis 37:2–34).

I wonder, did Joseph believe God would still be with him—protecting him, granting him favor, and allowing him to flourish despite his dire circumstances? Then when he arrived in a foreign country as a slave, did he ever imagine that serving his new master wholeheartedly for years would result in him being thrown in prison for resisting the sexual advances from his master's wife? How did Joseph process the bitter bile of betrayal again? It seems the more honest and righteous he acted, the worse he was treated by those God placed around him.

Fast-forward more than twenty years: Joseph was reunited with his brothers. They didn't even recognize Joseph as the highly appointed Egyptian official who held their lives and the lives of their families in his hands. As they bowed down at the brink of starvation, begging to buy food, did Joseph's dreams as a seventeen-year-old come flooding back to him?

> God allowed the eternal hem to be lifted to reveal that his divine plan is always greater than our sin.

In wisdom, Joseph then tested his brothers to see if twenty years of guilt had softened their hard hearts. Somehow, by God's mercy and sovereignty, his brothers passed the test. It was then that Joseph revealed himself to them. Their eyes were opened to God's providential plan that despite their wicked actions, God worked all things out for good (Genesis 45:4–5) as Joseph lovingly spoke to them:

> "God sent me before you to preserve for you a remnant on earth, and to keep alive for you many survivors. So it was not you who sent me here, but God. He has made me a father to Pharaoh, and lord of all his house and ruler over all the land of Egypt. Hurry and go up to my father and say to him, 'Thus says your son Joseph, God has made me lord of all Egypt. Come down to me; do not tarry. As for you, you meant evil against me, but God meant it for good, to bring it about that many people should be kept alive, as they are today.'" (Genesis 45:7–9, 50:20).

Joseph's older brothers must have been speechless at his testimony. In his suffering as a slave and prisoner, Joseph still saw the hand of God at work despite the wicked acts of his brothers. God used their malevolence to save all the surrounding nations. God allowed the eternal hem to be lifted to reveal that his divine plan is always greater than our sin.

God doesn't waste one sinful or righteous act in our life. He uses them all for good, either in the present or for eternity. God redeemed Joseph's times of suffering. He refined him into a great leader during his times as a slave and prisoner.

Joseph continued to trust God and act righteously despite the evil and betrayal swirling around him.

Most importantly, God saved the family of Israel (Jacob) because a remnant, Jesus Christ, would be born in the lineage of Judah. Jesus would step down from his heavenly kingdom, humble himself, become man, and live a perfect life. He would also experience betrayal, die a horrific death paying our debt as the complete sacrifice for all our sins, and then in three days rise from the dead to confirm our acquittal of salvation before God (Romans 4:25).[2]

> God doesn't waste one sinful or righteous act in our life. He uses them all for good, either in the present or for eternity.

Jesus did all of this in utter humility so that through our faith in him as our Savior, we would be reconciled with a holy God and enjoy the blessings of eternal life. Joseph's and Jesus' sufferings and betrayal were *not* wasted—they were ordained and an integral part of God's divine plan. Joseph's was to save the physical lives of everyone alive during that time; Jesus' was to save the eternal lives of all humanity.

Jesus' betrayal was even more heinous than Joseph's. Jesus was innocent. Joseph was prideful and arrogant. Joseph was betrayed by his eleven brothers, while Jesus was betrayed by someone closer than family: his disciple, Judas Iscariot, one of his closest companions. For over three years, Judas lodged, ate, and drank with Jesus, witnessing miracles by Jesus' hand: the healing of the sick, the blind made to see, the raising of the dead, walking on water, feeding the multitudes with a child's meal, casting out demons, quelling storms, and so many other miracles. Yet Judas sold his Redeemer, King, and God in the flesh for the price of a slave: thirty insignificant pieces of silver (Matthew 26:15), or the equivalent of $90.[3]

The most heart-wrenching part is that Jesus *knew* beforehand that Judas was going to betray him and would be responsible for his torture and horrific death. Judas planned all this before he sat down and ate the Last Supper, the Passover meal, with his Teacher, his Rabbi, the Savior of the world and the Son of God. He even dipped his bread into the same plate of wine as Jesus and asked if he would be the one to betray him. Jesus, his sights locked on eternity, calmly replied, "'You have said so'" (Matthew 26:25).

My favorite part of the night is during the Passover dinner, when Jesus does the unthinkable:

> *Jesus, knowing that the Father had given all things into his hands*, and that he had come from God and was going back to God, rose from supper. He laid aside his outer garments, and taking a towel, tied it around his waist. Then he poured water into a basin and *began to wash the disciples' feet and to wipe them with the towel that was wrapped around him.* (John 13:3–5 emphasis mine)

The act of washing someone's feet was considered extremely demeaning. It was an action performed by someone in submission and *only* by a Gentile slave, not a Hebrew or Hebrew slave and *never* by any person in authority, such as a rabbi or teacher. What always gives me pause is that Jesus, with a towel wrapped around his waist like a servant, washed *all* the disciples' feet, including Judas's. The Son of God humbled himself to one of the lowest of acts imaginable and washed his betrayer's feet. He, being sinless, did this so we, as sinners, wouldn't be tempted in self-righteousness thinking that any act of servitude is beneath us (John 12:1–17). And if God incarnate, Jesus Christ, was not unscathed by the sting of treason, why then should we be exempt?

In the garden of Gethsemane later that same evening, when Judas came with a throng of temple officers to arrest the Savior of the world, Jesus calmly asked him, "'Judas, would you betray the Son of Man with a kiss?'" (Luke 22:48).

By identifying his Lord with a kiss, Judas delivered Jesus to several rigged religious courts and then a public government trial. Jesus, although guiltless, was sentenced to death by Pontius Pilate, the Roman leader. Jesus was then scourged: stripped and whipped on the back with leather straps with pieces of bones, metal, and stones used to tear away the skin to pierce the skeletal muscles, which incited circulatory shock.[4] Then he was forced to carry his one-hundred-pound crossbar[5] through town. And finally, Jesus, even though innocent, was crucified: a slow death by suffocation by having the prisoner's hands and feet nailed to a Roman cross until there was no strength left in the legs to lift the body up to breathe.[6]

And if God incarnate, Jesus Christ, was not unscathed by the sting of treason, why then should we be exempt?

Jesus was not exempt from the pain of this world and instead received it all, so that he could draw near us and comfort us in our affliction:

> Since then we have a great high priest who has passed through the heavens, Jesus, the Son of God, let us hold fast our confession. For we do not have a high priest who is unable to sympathize with our weaknesses, but one who in every respect has been tempted as we are, yet without sin." (Hebrews 4:14–15)

As we see with Joseph and Jesus, the agony of betrayal runs deep. King David also experienced this pain as he cried out to God when his beloved son Absalom turned on him, demanding his father's blood and kingdom (2 Samuel 15–19):

> My heart is in anguish within me; the terrors of death have fallen upon me. Fear and trembling come upon me, and horror overwhelms me. And I say, "Oh, that I had wings like a dove! I would fly away and be at rest; yes, I would wander far away; I would lodge in the wilderness; I would hurry to find a shelter from the raging wind and tempest." For it is not an enemy who taunts me—then I could bear it; it is not an adversary who deals insolently with me—then I could hide from him. *But it is you, a man, my equal, my companion, my familiar friend.* We used to take sweet counsel together; within God's house we walked in the throng. My companion stretched out his hand against his friends; he violated his covenant. His speech was smooth as butter, yet war was in his heart; his words were softer than oil, yet they were drawn swords. *Cast your burden on the LORD, and*

> *he will sustain you; he will never permit the righteous to be moved.* (Psalm 55:4–8, 12–14, 20–22 emphasis mine)

The wounds from the dagger of betrayal are the most piercing when it's held in the hands of a loved one—a dear friend or family member like a parent, spouse, sibling, or a child. Those lacerations do the most damage and take the longest to heal.

I admire King David's transparency as he reveals his heart to God and runs to him in extreme suffering. We know that even though our friends, family, and loved ones might fail us, God will never forget us in our suffering; rather, he will always provide a way out in his perfect timing. Thankfully, the Lord is near to those who have and are suffering from the pain of betrayal…

I Know Your Pain

"Blessed are the poor in spirit, for theirs is the kingdom of heaven. Blessed are those who mourn, for they shall be comforted. Blessed are the meek, for they shall inherit the earth. Blessed are those who hunger and thirst for righteousness, for they shall be satisfied. Blessed are the merciful, for they shall receive mercy. Blessed are the pure in heart, for they shall see God. Blessed are the peacemakers, for they shall be called sons of God. Blessed are those who are persecuted for righteousness' sake, for theirs is the kingdom of heaven. Blessed are you when others revile you and persecute you and utter all kinds of evil against you falsely on my account. Rejoice and be glad, for your reward is great in heaven, for so they persecuted the prophets who were before you'" (Matthew 5:3–12).

Draw near to me, child, for I am all too familiar with the unfathomable depth of your pain from betrayal. I know your pain all too well. My chosen people have repeatedly forgotten me, they have whored after false gods in a feeble attempt to fill their hearts. They have thrown away their love to vain idols and the vanities of man. For "I have loved you with an everlasting love" (Jeremiah 31:3). I have paid a great price for you. I have bought you at the bride price of my one and only Son's blood. I have completely overpaid the redemptive value for your life. Your sins are paid in full. Yet why do you still chase after things that do not satisfy you?

"Why do you spend your money for that which is not bread, and your labor for that which does not satisfy? Listen diligently to me, and eat what is good, and delight yourselves in rich food" (Isaiah 55:2).

"Delight yourself in me and I will give you the desires of your heart" (Psalm 37:4).

There is nothing on this earth that will satisfy or remove your pain. Again, I intimately know your pain of betrayal. Come to me. Eat. Drink. Receive a fresh outpouring of my Spirit. Refill yourself in my love. Inhale *me*. Put away your wicked sexual acts, wine, strong drink, and elicit substances that destroy your body, mind, and soul. Turn from your natural inclinations to pacify yourself with the approval of man, anger, bitterness, wickedness, and love of mammon, for they profit nothing. The fruit of those vices, although initially appealing, turn sour in your stomach after your feeble immersion in them to mitigate your pain.

Come to me. Lay your burden at *my cross*. See with fresh eyes the price I paid for you. Fix your gaze upon my cross. Lay your hands on the hard, worn wood of my deathbed. Behold where *all* my wrath was completely poured out for your sins.

It is finished. You can come to *me*. Come to *me* with your hardened hearts; I will give you hearts of flesh.

Come to *me* all those who are weary and need rest.

My comfort will fill the hole inside of you.

Come to *me*. Rest in *me*.

I am your God.

You are my chosen, precious child.

Come.

Thankfully, God profoundly knows the life-shattering pain from betrayal. He is the only one who can fill the God-sized hole in your heart from treason. The only true healing possible to recover from this heinous act is found at the cross. Jesus has experienced your pain. Go to him. Run to him. Invite him to help you. He alone *will* comfort you. He will give you the strength to forgive and move forward. It's only through his grace on the cross that we can receive his peace that truly comforts us and transcends all understanding.

There are some people you might know who are mired in anger and unforgiveness. Atrocious acts have been committed against them, and they have dug deeper into their cocoon of bitterness. They might say things like, "But you don't know what they did to me, my family, my loved one, my gender, my race, and my innocence! The acts were too evil, abhorrent, and hateful. There is no way I can forgive *them*!"

I would agree. I don't know the details or the horrific things they experienced. But there is someone who does—God. He keeps each of our tears in a bottle like a vial of precious gems. He is the God of seeing. He sees all. He sees our pain and intimately knows what happened. And he feels our agony. He is a compassionate God. He is love. He is an amazing God. He loves us enough to send his one and only Son to pay the penalty in full for our sins. We were once God's enemy because of our sins. Each one of our sins is a personal betrayal against him.

Only through Jesus can we approach his holy throne of grace for comfort, compassion, and care. None of this healing salve is available anywhere in the flesh; it's only found in God. And this is my prayer …

Dear God,

Draw near to those who are reading this. Breathe on them. Let them see the holes in your hands, your feet, and your side—all received in full payment for their sins. Have them see and know deeply in their heart the great payment you made for their eternal life. Help them see they were bought for a price, a tremendous price, one they could never repay. Have them see their sins against you as *so* much greater than the sins committed against them. Heal their pain.

Please comfort them now by your Holy Spirit. Draw near to them. Fill them with your light. Convict them of their sins of self-righteousness as with the same thoughts they also condemn themselves.

Help them see their need to repent.

Help them forgive those who have sinned against them.

Help them *not* compare themselves to those who have sinned against them, but have them instead compare themselves to you, Jesus, who lived a perfect and sinless life so they could be forgiven.

Help them count the pennies of their $1,000,000,000 debt against you that you so readily forgave them for *their* sins—not contend and ruminate over the pennies of the $10,000 debt that was committed against them.

Help them *lift their gaze* to you, their extraordinary God and Savior—you who are so amazing, so beyond our limited, and finite comprehension.

For you are love.

Help those who are struggling to forgive to show your love and extend forgiveness when it is completely undeserved. Strengthen them to forgive the unforgivable and illuminate you, Lord Jesus, so that all who are watching will see *you* in *them*. Glorify your name through their acts of forgiveness. *Lift our gaze.*

It's only by your grace that we can forgive. It's only by your grace that we can live in obedience, despite how we feel.

Pour your Holy Spirit into us. Change our hard hearts of unbelief to soft, supple hearts of forgiveness and love. Allow us to be tools in your hands by extending forgiveness, especially to those who don't deserve it, those just like us, who you so readily forgave.

Forgive us for being like the unforgiving wicked servant. Pardon us for our self-righteousness. Absolve us for our transgressions.

Glorify your name. Use us as living billboards of grace to those who don't deserve it.

Bless us, oh God, with forgiving hearts.

We need you. We are your children.

In Jesus' name, I pray.

Amen.

APPLICATION QUESTIONS

Getting to the Heart of It

1. Have you ever experienced the pain of betrayal? Describe.

2. Have you forgiven this person (never replaying the act repeatedly to yourself, neither speaking about it to others nor bringing it up again in conversation)? Do you understand this sin or debt against you was only an infinitesimal fraction of what you have been forgiven for by Jesus Christ? Why or why not?

3. Write down your prayer for the person responsible for the betrayal of your trust, whom you need to forgive.

4. Read Matthew 18:21–35 aloud. How are you like the wicked servant?

5. Is there anyone you are withholding forgiveness from that you need to repent to God, and to them, for your sin of unforgiveness? List the people God is revealing to you.

6. How are we all like Joseph's brothers and Judas with our desperate need to be reconciled with and forgiven by God?

7. How have you personally witnessed the power of forgiveness in your life, both as a receiver and as a granter? Describe.

8. How are we, who were once enemies of God, just like (or even worse than) those who have sinned against us?

"Call to me and I will answer you and *tell you great and unsearchable things you do not know.*"

~ Jeremiah 33:3 NIV *emphasis mine*

1. Before presenting your prayer requests to God, remind yourself of whom you are praying to. List five different attributes of God you haven't listed yet.

   1 ______
   2 ______
   3 ______
   4 ______
   5 ______

2. Then list at least five additional blessings (that you haven't listed before) in your life that you are grateful for.

   1 ______
   2 ______
   3 ______
   4 ______
   5 ______
   ______

3. List your prayer requests.

4. Write down anything else the Lord is speaking to your heart.

5. Finally, close by praising God in advance for whatever the outcome.

CHAPTER EIGHT

Amazing Grace

"O death, where is your victory? O death, where is your sting?"
~ 1 Corinthians 15:55

The little blue line on the simple white stick gave me such joy. It meant I was pregnant! I already knew it in my heart though; I was craving cheeseburgers like a lunatic, a clear indication that I was with child.

Every part of me was glowing as I showed my husband the proof. He couldn't stop grinning. We had been unsuccessful in getting pregnant for over a year. Since we were in our forties, we had been forced into the painful fertility-testing-and-treatment gauntlet. Exhausted from the discouraging results, stress, and pressure, I had stopped all the treatments and testings a month earlier. I prayed that if God wanted me pregnant, he'd have to do it by himself, without the procedures. Now without any medical assistance, I was pregnant and jubilant! God had heard and answered my prayers.

With a spring in my step, I went to the doctor's office and had the confirming blood work done. That little kit I had purchased at the drugstore was correct. I was pregnant! This was a beautiful anniversary gift from God to my husband and me. I thanked and praised God all the way home.

About two weeks later, I started bleeding heavily. Immediately I called the doctor. I still remember that conversation. Without even seeing me, the nurse told me in a soft voice, "I'm so sorry. It's a loss."

I blubbered into the phone, "What? How can you be so sure? Isn't there a test you can do?"

With a gentle and understanding tone, she said, "Sure, you can come in for blood work. We can do a blood test for the pregnancy hormones, but at this point be prepared that your pregnancy is a loss."

I called my husband right away. We were devastated. He lovingly convinced me to go in for more bloodwork.

My world was spinning. How did this happen? After all, God made me pregnant without fertility treatments. And then he did so only for us to lose the child? Why would he do this? Wasn't he sovereign?

I had no words to describe the depth of emotions I was experiencing. I was terrified that I was losing my baby and there was nothing I could do to stop it.

Angrily, I drove to the doctor's office. I cried as they took my blood. They called me first thing the next day. I was still bleeding. The bloodwork confirmed it was a loss; my baby had died.

Eight years before, I had been pregnant and given birth to a healthy child, so I knew what the baby looked like at this gestation age. I remembered the little seahorse-shaped being who was so tiny and helpless on the ultrasound monitor. It even had a heartbeat within the first weeks of conception. It was a baby. And now, "*It was a loss*"? That little baby I had waited for, prayed for, cried out to God for, was gone. He or she was here one day and then gone, just like that.

The sense of bereavement I felt was so profound, it shocked me. I was completely unprepared for the depth of grief that encompassed me. My heart physically ached for my unborn child. Scripture did little to comfort me. I had to forcibly push those words of truth down from my head to my heart. It was like trying to swallow a large hunk of dry, hard bread without chewing it completely; it just seemed to get stuck like a golf ball in my throat.

Sometimes the agony was too much—it just seemed to weigh down heavily on my chest, constricting my air passages. During those dark days, all my senses numbed. I was living in a fog. Nothing smelled good, food had lost its taste, and everything seemed to hurt. Comfort from the physical realm completely eluded me.

My husband was very supportive. He continually prayed for me and held me when I couldn't sleep at night. My Christian brothers and sisters were wonderful as they tried to comfort me. I would smile and nod as they gently pointed me to God and implored me to look to him in my despair. On the inside, I felt like a part of me was dying. I felt they had no clue of the intensity of my suffering and they were attempting to place a small bandage over my hemorrhaging heart. Sometimes, I falsely believed my loss was too great even for God to reach. During those painful moments, people's attempts to assuage me just seemed to roll off like water on a duck's back.

Desperately, I would read the promises in Scripture, repeatedly, like a child over chewing a large piece of taffy. I found some temporary comfort in Isaiah when he refers to our Savior as the one who:

> Was despised and rejected by men; a man of sorrows, and acquainted with grief; and as one from whom men hide their faces he was despised, and we esteemed

> him not. Surely he has borne our griefs and carried our sorrows; yet we esteemed him stricken, smitten by God, and afflicted. (Isaiah 53:3–4)

If the Son of God was not exempt from the agony of suffering, then why should I be? This gave me strength to go to church even though I felt like I was trudging through quicksand. Devoid of sensation, I had a hard time standing and lifting my hands up to God in worship. It was painful to look to God who, in his infinite goodness and wisdom, decided it was better for our baby to be with him instead of us. I shuffled away from the Sunday service deeply immersed in sorrow.

> If the Son of God was not exempt from the agony of suffering, then why should I be?

The next Sunday I once again went to church with my family. I winced as everyone hugged me, told me they loved me, and said that they were praying for us, especially for me. When worship started, tears just rolled down my cheeks. But this time it was different.

Everything stood still.

It was then I saw it…

Amazing Grace

I saw him. He was undeniable. Jesus was standing there in all his glory, his beauty, and his purity. He was in front of a backdrop of a breathtaking view of heaven, but it paled in comparison to his holiness. He was absolutely glorious.

It was Jesus Christ, and he was just standing there, holding a little girl's hand. She had the most beautiful long brown wavy hair down her back and glistening hazel eyes with perfectly placed sparks of gold. Her eyes looked intently at me. Compassion emulated from them. With a tilt of her head, she gently tossed her hair from her shoulders to reveal the soft highlights that reflected the pure radiance of the heaven.

She looked down at me in concern. She looked up at Jesus' warm loving eyes and softly said, "*Mommy doesn't understand, does she*?"

Jesus smiled back at her and then lovingly looked at me and said, "No, she doesn't yet. But she will." Jesus then picked her up and held her as a parent would comfort a child. This beautiful little girl then wrapped her arms and legs around Jesus, nuzzled her face into his neck and inhaled his glory. It was such a beautiful sight. As she slightly turned her face back to me, cradled in her Savior's arms, I saw her smile with her eyes closed in complete comfort, peace and tranquility.

She lifted her head, looked down at me again, and said to her Savior, "*Mommy is still so sad.*" Jesus nodded and laid his hand on my shoulder.

It was then that all my grief left me.

It exited in a rush through my right shoulder where his hand rested upon me.

The darkness was completely gone. I was at peace. My baby was with Jesus in heaven. My baby was safe. My baby was saved. She was in her Savior's arms. Wasn't that the answer to all my prayers I would have prayed over her all her life? *Who was to decree this child should live one extra day either inside or outside of my womb?* This child was God's, not mine.

This child's days were numbered, as were the very hairs on her head.

God gives life and takes it away. It was his decision on the number of her days, not mine. And most importantly, my child was with Jesus. My child, my little love, the one that I would never hold in this world, is now in eternity with God. She is saved from God's wrath.

Hallelujah!

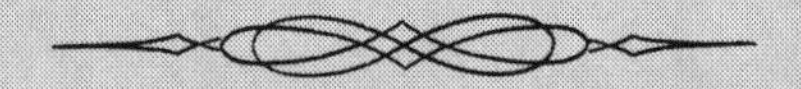

Then a peace that surpasses all human understanding washed over me like a tidal wave. I started chanting, "God is infinitely wise. He is my God, my Comfort, and my Strength. He is my everything. I am at peace." The image of my child in Jesus' arms gave me such intense solace.

It was only after the touch on my shoulder that I was able to praise him. As I had both of my arms raised, the pastor who led worship abruptly stopped playing the current song and broke out into an unplanned hymn. The band members fumbled but then adapted to the insertion in the song list. The lyrics for "Amazing Grace" popped up on the large screens above the band as the worship leader's voice resonated deeply with my soul:

Amazing grace! How sweet the sound
That saved a wretch like me!
I once was lost, but now am found;
Was blind, but now I see.
'Twas grace that taught my heart to fear,
and grace my fears relieved;
How precious did that grace appear
the hour I first believed.
Through many dangers, toils and snares,
I have already come;
'Tis grace hath brought me safe thus far,
and grace will lead me home.[1]

God is so kind. "Amazing Grace" is still one of my favorite hymns. Those haunting lyrics and melody have always comforted me. It seems most funerals I attend incorporate it somewhere in the service.

This time that song was beyond a healing salve to my pain; it gave me hope. The worship band only played a few verses, but for me it was more than enough. It was a private memorial service for my baby who was now resting on Jesus' chest. There is no place I would rather her to be! Now I was able to praise God in complete trust for losing our child.

Death is the one thing all of us share and will experience at one time. It is unavoidable. No matter what we do, we will all die. Most of us in our lifetime will experience the loss of someone we hold precious. Other types of losses are heart-breaking as well: the elimination of a job, career, relationship, marriage, lifestyle, home, finances, freedom, health, circle of supporting friends, or the estrangement from a family member. Some people experience multiple losses at one time. No matter the cause, the end of something we treasure creates a flood of sorrow in our hearts.

It's usually during that first year when your precious memories become your enemy. The holidays, birthdays, anniversaries, work events, community activities, church, and certain smells or foods can all be innocent culprits. Surprisingly, they rip open shallow, newly healed wounds of sorrow at the worst possible moments. We can be walking through the grocery store when we see our loved one's favorite snack food and become suddenly overwhelmed by an emotional deluge. Unfortunately, that's normal (yet embarrassing) in the grieving process.

Sometimes it seems certain people have a better handle on grieving than others. They seem to bounce back to their joyful, happy life rather quickly, while others seem to wade through the process more slowly. They can become incapacitated by the dark, heavy cloud that enveloped them, cutting them off from the world. Some of us get stuck in a state of numbness. We're just going about our days blindly, placing one foot in front of the other. We don't realize how emotionally detached we are from those who are closest to us.

The stages of grief, invited or not, can take up permanent residency. The voyage through denial, bargaining, anger, depression, and acceptance is not an easy one. It can demolish the sense of peace, love, and joy we took for granted in days past.

> I lift up my eyes to the hills. From where does my help come? My help comes from the Lord, who made heaven and earth.
>
> ~ Psalm 121:1–2

Whatever your response is as you process the loss of someone or something you held dear, it is a true faith-testing season. When I'm wading through especially deep waters, these verses remind me of God's faithfulness:

> The Lord is near to the brokenhearted and saves the crushed in spirit (Psalm 34:18). Count it all joy, my brothers, when you meet trials of various kinds, for you know that the testing of your faith produces steadfastness. And let steadfastness have its full effect, that you may be perfect and complete, lacking in nothing. (James 1:2–4)

Depending on the depth of the valley of death we're walking through, the act of lifting our gaze and applying Scripture to the deep chasm of pain in our heart can be beyond comprehension. King David encapsulated these emotions as he experienced several intense seasons of suffering. Instead of wallowing in his grief, he cried out to God, "I lift up my eyes to the hills. From where does my help come? My help comes from the Lord, who made heaven and earth" (Psalm 121:1–2).

God is keenly aware of our grief. He is closest to us during our darkest times. He keeps count of our tosses in bed, he catches our tears in a bottle and records them in his book (Psalm 56:8). All our days are numbered (Psalm 139:16), as are the very hairs on our head (Matthew 10:30). God is intricately involved in every aspect of our being, even our emotions. He sees our suffering; he is not immune to it. Jesus even proclaimed a blessing over those who are in sorrow: "Blessed are those who mourn, for they shall be comforted" (Matthew 5:4).

Jesus came not to sympathize, but to empathize with our suffering.

Jesus also personally experienced the pain from the passing of a loved one in one of the shortest and most powerful portions of Scripture. When Jesus was told that his beloved friend, Lazarus, had died, "Jesus wept" (John 11:35). Jesus knew that he was going to raise Lazarus from the dead, even as tears ran down his cheeks while he walked to the tomb. Some commentaries believe that tears slid down Jesus' face not because of his own personal grief over his friend's death, but because he deeply felt the agonizing hearts of those near him.[2] Jesus came not to sympathize, but to empathize with our suffering.

Remember, Jesus allowed his dear friend Lazarus to die and for Lazarus' family to experience the anguish of grief. He waited until Lazarus was dead for four days and started to decompose (John 11:39) before he started his two-day journey to see him. *Jesus purposely delayed, so the power of God could be glorified, not just to the family, but to the entire town.*

When pressed by the grieving family why he didn't come sooner and heal Lazarus, he simply replied, "'Lazarus has died, and for your sake I am glad that I was not there, so that you may believe'" (John 11:14–15) because, "Many of the Jews therefore, who had come with Mary and had seen what he did, believed in him" (John 11:45).

How often does God do that with us? He allows us to suffer for a greater purpose—one that is not seen at the time, but revealed later. For that is the very essence of faith: being sure of what we hope for. It is being certain of what we do not see (Hebrews 11:1 NIrV).

During an intense period of a trial in my life, I poured out my heart to God and prayed fervently, "Oh Lord, hear my prayers. You know the desires of my heart. Please don't tarry." The Lord responded gently, "Do I ever tarry? And if I do, it is to bring about a greater good so that I might be glorified." I tearfully praised him for withholding reprieve from my anguish.

> "Do I ever tarry? And if I do, it is to bring about a greater good so that I might be glorified."
>
> ~ God

If you think God is lingering in answering your prayers, rest in the knowledge that he is not done working all things for good for everyone involved. Because Lazarus's family already believed in him, Jesus waited for Lazarus to pass and begin decaying (John 11:39) before he raised him from the dead, so that the net of salvation would be cast on a larger audience.

It is the same with us. God allows us to go through trials so the power of his risen Son can be glorified to everyone around us. Usually we are so embroiled in our own personal misery that we're unaware of the multitude God has providentially placed around us. These are the same people who are watching us, loving us, and emotionally upholding us while we walk through our dark times. Each season of suffering has been sovereignly designed by a loving God so that all can see and even taste how Jesus meets us, comforts us, and gives us the strength to lift our gaze.

> The good news is this: the time we spend in the deep waters of sorrow is temporary and *will* pass.

Then when God, in his loving kindness, pours out a deluge of his Holy Spirit and we receive his deep soul-satisfying peace, the rippling salvation effect brings revival to even the hardest hearts, saving them from the eternal fires of hell. God is therefore glorified beyond our wildest imaginations.

The good news is this: the time we spend in the deep waters of sorrow is temporary and *will* pass. And the even better news is as a believer in Jesus Christ, any suffering we experience on earth is the closest to an eternity in hell that we will ever face. This is all because we are reconciled with a holy God through our faith in Jesus as our personal Savior.

If you are suffering or have suffered from loss, this is my prayer for you …

Dear God,

Draw close to those who are reading this. Wrap your loving arms around them. Comfort them. Remove the affliction of grief from them. Help them *lift their gaze* to you. Keep them single-focused on your goodness, love, and mercy. Pour out your Spirit upon them.

Whether they are a seasoned worker or one of your new hires, bless them with your peace that transcends all understanding. I pray that if they do not yet have a saving knowledge of you, drop the scales from their eyes. Allow them to see their desperate need for you as their Savior for their sins. Comfort them with your cross. Permit them to see the nail holes in Jesus' hands and feet and the gash in his side, which is just a sampling of the great price paid for them. You did all of this so that through faith in your Son they will have unlimited access to you, their God and Father.

Bless them with the gift of repentance. Have them turn from their sins and declare that you are their God. For you are the only way. For their faith in you as their Savior, Jesus, is their only protection from the eternal agony from an everlasting lake of fire in hell.

Just as you instructed Moses to have all the Israelites place the blood of a spotless lamb over their doorposts for protection, cover all of us who claim Jesus as our Savior, with your blood. For when the angel of death came that first Passover night in Egypt and took the lives of all the firstborn sons in the homes that did not have the blood of lamb on them, place that same blood upon us who claim you, Jesus, as our protector and Savior. In doing so, we receive you as our refuge and strength, and are no longer subject to the eternal wrath of God for our sins.

Allow us to receive the confirmation that you have paid the just penalty of eternal suffering for all our sins. Wash us with your blood so that our sins, once crimson, are now white as freshly driven snow as we are forgiven and washed clean. For as Moses, a murderer, was passed over from judgment, so will you pass over those that are covered by the blood of the one and only true Lamb of God.

For we are all sinners and desperately need salvation from our sins. Lift all feelings of despair, hopelessness, and dread from us and our hearts.

Cover us with the blood of Jesus. Pour out your Spirit upon us.

Touch our shoulders, dear God. Remove from us our grief, profound sense of loss, and season for suffering as far as the east is from the west.

Bless us, oh Lord and King, with your peace. Draw near to us. Comfort the afflicted and those who mourn.

Lift our gaze to you, and keep our focus on you despite our circumstances and heavy hearts. Pour out liquid love into us so that we have inexplicable joy in our trials.

Show us your favor, your blessing, and your love that only comes through faith in your Son, Jesus Christ. Have all who are around us clearly see, hear, smell and taste your presence in their life.

Show them just a glimpse of the wonders of your mercy and love, which are all available to us through Jesus.

Bless us, oh Lord.

In Jesus' precious name, I pray.

Amen.

Oh, but Jesus! Jesus who was no stranger to trials, betrayals, and suffering, yet he did not sin in unbelief of God's sovereignty, rule, and knowledge that the Father is always good. That same Jesus comforts us in our dark days.

And oh, that cross! When we wrap our arms and legs around the cross and lay our hot burning cheek on it, we realize that old rugged cross is now smooth, like a piece of driftwood, from the tears of suffering from those who have gone before us. The very thing we think would never provide solace, an instrument of torture and a vision of horror, now becomes the only thing that can comfort us.

Allow Jesus' complete work on the cross to lift your gaze.

Your Savior loves you.

He died for you.

He will not withhold one good gift from you.

Draw near to him in your suffering.

Rest your grieving head on that soft piece of wood of the cross.

He alone will comfort you; God is faithful.

APPLICATION QUESTIONS

Getting to the Heart of It

1. Describe a time when you experienced a loss and how you got through it.

2. Did you get stuck in any stage of grief or emotion such as denial, bargaining, anger, depression, or acceptance? Describe.

3. Have you ever asked anyone to pray for you when you were suffering? If so, elaborate on the outcome.

4. List your favorite Bible stories or Scriptures that comfort you.

5. Have you ever been able to praise God in worship during a trial? If so, describe your experience.

6. Specifically, how are you assured that God deeply cares for you, even in your times of grief or suffering?

Let us then approach God's throne of grace with confidence, so that we may receive mercy and find grace to help us in our time of need.

~ HEBREWS 4:16 NIV *emphasis mine*

1. Before presenting your prayer requests to God, remind yourself of whom you are praying to. List five new attributes of God you haven't listed yet.

   1 ______________________________
   2 ______________________________
   3 ______________________________
   4 ______________________________
   5 ______________________________

2. Then list at least five additional blessings (ones you haven't listed before) in your life that you are grateful for.

   1 ______________________________
   2 ______________________________
   3 ______________________________
   4 ______________________________
   5 ______________________________

3. List your prayer requests.

4. Write down anything else the Lord is speaking to your heart.

5. Finally, close by praising God in advance for whatever the outcome.

SECTION III

Our Response

CHAPTER NINE

Know Who Fights for You

Then Amalek came and fought with Israel at Rephidim. So Moses said to Joshua, "Choose for us men, and go out and fight with Amalek. Tomorrow I will stand on the top of the hill with the staff of God in my hand." So Joshua did as Moses told him, and fought with Amalek, while Moses, Aaron, and Hur went up to the top of the hill. Whenever Moses held up his hand, Israel prevailed, and whenever he lowered his hand, Amalek prevailed. But Moses's hands grew weary, so they took a stone and put it under him, and he sat on it, while Aaron and Hur held up his hands, one on one side, and the other on the other side. *So his hands were steady until the going down of the sun.* And Joshua overwhelmed Amalek and his people with the sword. Then the LORD said to Moses, "Write this as a memorial in a book and recite it in the ears of Joshua, that I will utterly blot out the memory of Amalek from under heaven." And Moses built an altar and called the name of it, *The Lord Is My Banner.*

~ EXODUS 17:8–15 *emphasis mine*

MY HEART SANK.

There blinking, was another notification, taunting me.

I sighed. I didn't want to open it.

You have to, I bravely thought to myself.

"No, I don't," I argued back.

Fingers hovering over the open button, I groaned inwardly as I started reading it in the preview pane. It was worse than I thought.

Heart heavy, I opened it and read it in its entirety. It was seething with rage and misspelled vulgarity. I would've been shocked if it wasn't the hundredth time I'd received an email like this one. They always came from the same source and were written in the same manner.

I learned over the years to not respond the same day. Waiting a day allowed me to pray for wisdom and for things to settle. Having responded hastily in the past, I'd been convicted by the Lord that I was accountable for my response to someone else's sin. The email went into my action file.

Before going back to the plethora of work emails, the Lord dropped a jewel of wisdom into my heart: "You are married now. This is no longer your responsibility; it is your husband's. Forward it to him."

Tilting my head as the corners of my mouth curled upward, I mumbled, "Now, *that* would be something."

I still hesitated before I emailed it to my husband. Knowing all parties involved, this could cause a war of epic proportions. But the Lord spoke firmly to my heart, "This needs to be done. Step out of this. I have given you a husband as your protector and kinsman redeemer. You need to stop fighting. The battle is not yours."

"Wow. Okay, then," I said firmly. And without hesitation, as directed, I forwarded the odious email to my husband.

A minute later, I got a phone call. My husband was horrified at the contents of the correspondence. "How long have you been getting these?" he demanded.

"Several years now," I replied with an eerie calmness.

"I'll handle things from here," he said with such strong headship, it surprised me. "Do not respond to any future emails. Forward all of them to me."

"Sure." I swallowed hard.

The email fusillade went on for a few days between my husband and my harasser. I kept getting nasty emails addressed only to me, which I obediently forwarded to my husband. My kinsman redeemer replied firmly, always copying me. My job was to pray.

"So is everything resolved?" I asked my husband a few days later over dinner.

"Not yet, but it will be. Cowards can't handle it when someone stands up to them. If I need to, I will go down to his office and speak to him man to man. No one should address another person like this, *especially my wife*. I told him so in my last email." My husband's steely eyes blazed with confidence.

"*What*? You're going down *there*? To his work?" I asked, my voice increasing in volume. "That's going to be ugly. Are you sure you want to even put that out *there*?"

"Yes. This has been going on too long. I'm your husband, and again, no one speaks to my wife that way. I don't care who they are!" He gave me that I'm-done-with-this-conversation look.

Hands up in surrender, I said with a smirk, "It's all yours to handle."

He dismissed me with a nod.

It took about a week, but the barrage of insulting emails decreased. Within a month they completely stopped.

Yes, I thought to myself, enjoying a break from the onslaught of vicious emails, *it* is *nice to have someone fight for you. Thank you, Lord.*

Thankfully, we as Christians have a God who fights our battles for us. Sometimes he sends us a Joshua (like my husband) to fight our battles for us in the flesh, while we like Moses are commanded to pray. Other times our only response is to pray and allow God to fight for us. Either way, our first and foremost response to a trial is to remember who goes before us and then respond accordingly.

When Moses erected this crude altar, he did it as a tangible reminder to the Israelites and all the other observing nations that in their first battle out of Egypt, the people of God were victorious[1] because of who went ahead of them.

In doing so, Moses declared a new season for the Israelites, who were no longer helpless slaves but now warriors. Their new marching orders were a reminder: "the battle is the Lord's; and that the standard under which you war is the God for whose cause you contend—none else and none less than Jehovah Himself. You are consecrated soldiers, set apart to fight for God."[3]

> "The battle is the Lord's; and that the standard under which you war is the God for whose cause you contend—none else and none less than Jehovah Himself. You are consecrated soldiers, set apart to fight for God."
>
> ~ Alexander MacLaren

The name of the altar, "The Lord Is My Banner" (Exodus 17:15) or "Jehovahnissi" (Exodus 17:15 KJV), also means "the Lord is my miracle."[3] A banner is always in front of the army and determines its direction. The foremost duty of every Christian warrior is absolute obedience to God's will, which is the total suppression of one's own will.

One commentary extrapolates, "In order to be blessed, to be strong, to be victorious, the indispensable condition is that our inmost desire shall be, 'Not my will, but Thine be done.'"[4] This humble posture of one's heart is only available through the grace of God. This resolve cannot be conjured up, applied, manipulated, or maintained by our own internal fortitude.

It is our job and response to fixate on "The Lord Is My Banner" or our "Jehovahnissi" when we are going through our battles. It reminds us of who is fighting for us. *Jehovah* is the Greek word for *Yahweh* in Hebrew, the very name God gave himself when he first introduced himself to Moses at the burning bush. It means "I AM WHAT I AM, or I WILL BE WHAT I WILL BE" (Exodus 3:14) or that God is the great I AM and is "eternal and unchangeable: the same yesterday, today, and forever."[5]

It is our job and response to fixate on "The Lord Is My Banner" or our "Jehovahnissi" when we are going through our battles.

The name Yahweh for God was, and still is today, among certain groups, considered too sacred to even speak or write. It also declares that God is the only God. In biblical times, the only person who could utter God's true name was the high priest on the Day of Atonement. The Jews reverently used the word *Adonai* or *Lord* in its place.

When God revealed himself with this name, he instructed Moses to tell the Israelites to use this name as their rescuer (Exodus 6:2–3). God liberated over two million Hebrews from centuries of cruel Egyptian bondage with *this* name. He was and is a jealous God, wanting all the glory to go to him—the great Jehovahnissi, which was, is, and will be the banner for his chosen people for generations.

Even today, we can claim the banner of our God, Jehovahnissi, in our battles. He goes ahead of us and fights for us. He allows trials to come only to strengthen us and draw us closer to him. It's our job to pray to him and trust him as he battles for us while we, his servants, obey his leading. In doing so, we need to remember who is our God …

Jehovahnissi

Who we flee to. *Who brings forth miracles.*
Who our God really is. *Who we are praying to.*
Who already has the victory. *Who will never reject us.*
Who is our comforter. *Who sees all things.*
Who holds all things *together in his hands.*
Who is sovereign over everything, *both seemingly good and bad.*
Who works all things out *for good and his glory.*
Who is our healer. *Who is our redeemer.*
Who is our provider. *Who is our Creator.*
Who we go to for peace. *Who fights for us.*
Who is the most *powerful force in the universe.*
Who is God Almighty. *Who we run to in times of trouble.*
And who is *our God.*

The young soon-to-be King David held these truths so deep in his heart that he was able to save the entire nation of Israel. He knew who went before him. David knew and trusted his God. He grasped beyond a shadow of a doubt that his people were the chosen elect of God. David realized that their God went before the Israelites. David comprehended that their living God kept everything in place: from the blood pumping through their veins to the planets, sun, and moon suspended in space. God holds *everything* in his hands and holds *all* things together (Colossians 1:17). If *that* God, the holy living God, is for us and fights for us, who can even stand against us?

I imagine that is exactly what David saw when he looked up to see the nearly ten-foot giant (1 Samuel 17:4 NIV) shouting insults at the Israelites on that battlefront. Every day for forty days, Goliath would haughtily bellow:

If *that* God, the holy living God is for us and fights for us, who can even stand against us?

> "Why do you come out and line up for battle? Am I not a Philistine, and are you not the servants of Saul? Choose a man and have him come down to me. If he is able to fight and kill me, we will become your subjects; but if I overcome him and kill him, you will become our subjects and serve us." Then the Philistine said, "This day I defy the armies of Israel! Give me a man and let us fight each other." On hearing the Philistine's words, Saul and all the Israelites were dismayed and terrified. (1 Samuel 17:8–11 NIV)

Upon hearing Goliath's tirade, David looked to his God. David's trial (this terrifying giant) looked puny next to David's *big* God.

A few days earlier, Jesse, David's father, had absolutely no idea that a history-altering event would involve his youngest son and a giant from the enemy's camp. He loaded up the shepherding David with enough bundles of roasted grain, loaves of bread, and cheese to fortify his older sons and all the officers. When David arrived, he was in disbelief that no one in the entire army would stand up to the mouthy Philistine hulk as he spewed vulgarities on the Israelites for the past forty days. Instead, they even scoffed among themselves:

> "Do you see how this man keeps coming out? He comes out to defy Israel. The king will give great wealth to the man who kills him. He will also give him his daughter in marriage and will exempt his family from taxes in Israel." (1 Samuel 17:25 NIV)

David, single-focused on his God and not on this barbaric titan, inquired:

> "What will be done for the man who kills this Philistine and removes this disgrace from Israel? *Who is this uncircumcised Philistine that he should defy the armies of the living God?*" (1 Samuel 17:25 NIV emphasis mine)

I love that part. It's as if David said to the army, "Who is *this* guy? Just look at him. He's nothing compared to our living God! I mean, *really*? And you all are terrified? Come on. *Seriously*?"

Even so, Goliath must have looked intimidating out there: snorting offensive insults, swinging around his humungous sword and his weavers-beam-sized staff, towering over every man in full gleaming-bronze battle gear that weighed more than several men. But David was locked on his God, not his trial or his enemy.

Then David's not-very-supportive brother, Eliab, entered the discord. He heard his little brother inquiring about Goliath and berated David publicly:

> "Why have you come down here? And with whom did you leave those few sheep in the wilderness? I know how conceited you are and how wicked your heart is; you came down only to watch the battle." (1 Samuel 17:28 NIV)

But David was locked on his God, not his trial or his enemy.

Eliab must have been convicted by David's faith. And David challenged Eliab's and the rest of the army's lack of bravery and manhood. Eliab tore down the only person who stepped out in faith to declare exactly whose battle this really was—God's. David's questions were the mirror that defied the Israelites' crowd mentality. They were operating from a place of fear, anxiety, and dread, and not one of trust in their holy, perfect, and almighty God.

I have always been impressed with David's firm response and respectful dismissal of his older brother:

> "Now what have I done?" said David. "Can't I even speak?" He then turned away to someone else and brought up the same matter, and the men answered him as before. (1 Samuel 17:29–30 NIV)

God, even today, is looking for the obedient few to step out in confidence to claim in advance Jehovahnissi's victory. The battle has already been won. God fights for his people.

God, even today, is looking for the obedient few to step out in confidence to claim in advance Jehovahnissi's victory. The battle has already been won.

Encouraged by the wave of God's providential hand, King Saul got wind of one single reed in his camp who was not bent by the wind of dread over Goliath and was standing firm. Saul, being a strategic general, sent for David. He wanted to discern this young man's heart firsthand. David's response to King Saul warms my heart (as I'm sure it did God's): "'Let no one lose heart on account of this Philistine; your servant will go and fight him'" (1 Samuel 17:32 NIV). King Saul, upon closer examination of this young shepherd, lost all hope. Saul exclaimed:

> "There's no way you can fight this Philistine and possibly win! You're only a boy, and he's been a man of war since his youth." (1 Samuel 17:33 NLT)

At this point, I envision David squaring his shoulders, puffing out his chest, and giving his king a steely look through those passionate eyes of his. He then reverently informed Saul:

> "Your servant has been keeping his father's sheep. When a lion or a bear came and carried off a sheep from the flock, I went after it, struck it and rescued the sheep from its mouth. When it turned on me, I seized it by its hair, struck it and killed it. Your servant has

> killed both the lion and the bear; this uncircumcised Philistine will be like one of them, because he has defied the armies of the living God. The LORD who rescued me from the paw of the lion and the paw of the bear will rescue me from the hand of this Philistine." (1 Samuel 17:34–37 NIV)

I can imagine the corners of King Saul's mouth turning upward in amusement as he just nodded in approval. He saw in David something he had not seen in himself or the rest of his army. He saw a warrior's heart. In wisdom, Saul then gave his kingly blessing to David to go out and fight the mighty ten-foot giant on the entire army's behalf. Saul encouraged David with excellent counsel for us all: "'Go, and the LORD be with you'" (1 Samuel 17:37 NIV).

As any good and wise military officer would do, Saul tried to loan David his battle armor. Saul's battle gear swam on the boyish David. David, still an adolescent, was too young to serve in Saul's army (Numbers 1:3). And Saul being a head taller than all the other Israelites (1 Samuel 10:23) was well-seasoned in hand-to-hand combat. David must have looked ridiculous dragging and clanging Saul's ill-fitting, well-worn, heavy suit of armor on the ground as he walked.

David wisely told Saul that he couldn't go into battle with someone else's battle gear and weapons. David decided to use what he was already familiar with, his trusty slingshot, a seemingly foolish weapon in response to Goliath's size, battle armor, and personal arsenal. He went to the riverbed and selected five smooth stones, then slid them into his

> Go, and the LORD be with you.
>
> ~ 1 SAMUEL 17:37 NIV

shepherd's pouch with the confidence that his God went before him in all things.

David's unwavering awareness was on his God, not his enemy or the battle. And with his sling firmly gripped in his hand, David separated himself from the cowardly Israelite army to challenge the enemy, defend his people, and glorify his God (1 Samuel 17:38–40). He boldly declared to his and God's enemy:

> "You come against me with sword and spear and javelin, but I come against you in the name of the LORD Almighty, the God of the armies of Israel, whom you have defied. This day the LORD will deliver you into my hands, and I'll strike you down and cut off your head. This very day I will give the carcasses of the Philistine army to the birds and the wild animals, and the whole world will know that there is a God in Israel. All those gathered here will know that it is not by sword or spear that the LORD saves; for the battle is the LORD's, and he will give all of you into our hands." (1 Samuel 17:45–47 NIV)

David, in faith, ran forward to the battle line (1 Samuel 17:48) and declared the victory in advance.

Goliath, arrogant in his own strength, moved closer to attack the small shepherd boy. David, in faith, ran forward to the battle line (1 Samuel 17:48) and declared the victory in advance. Reaching into his bag, he simply took out the first stone, mounted it, and slung it. Miraculously it struck the giant Philistine right in the head, sinking deeply into his forehead. I often wonder if a mighty archangel's thumb pushed that stone farther into Goliath's head, thereby sealing the end of this season of tyranny by the Philistines.

This once seemingly insurmountable ten-foot enemy fell face down on the ground with an earth-shattering thud (1 Samuel 17:49 NIV). David, without hesitation, ran over and cut off the giant's head with Goliath's *own* sword, confirming God's promise over his people as the one and only true God, the great Jehovahnissi.

After the dust settled, the Israelites annihilated the Philistine army, plundering their camp with loud shouting (1 Samuel 17:52 NIV). What an amazing account of God's faithfulness! He lifted the weak and claimed triumph for himself through the actions of one obedient, faith-filled shepherd boy. God doesn't call the equipped, he equips the called (Hebrews 13:21 NIV). And if David can triumphantly face his seemingly invincible, more experienced ten-foot enemy, what more can we do if we, like David, obediently step out in faith trusting explicitly in our God?

How often do we try to put on other people's faith and apply their life experiences to our situation? We attempt to follow their exact footprints like a treasure map to get what we think we want. God has given each one of us unique abilities to defeat our enemy. We can't wear anyone else's armor into war. What weapons worked for them in their battle might not work for us.

Also, we should remember not to judge others as they are walking in their obedience to God's Word. What God uses in one person's life is usually very different from what he uses in our life.

God hand-selects your battle and your five smooth stones particularly for you. Then he bestows on you your perfectly fitting battle gear. It has been handcrafted exclusively for you and your battle. They

> You do not comprehend the power in which you pray to, or the one who paid such a high price for you. If you did, you would be living victoriously, focusing only on your God.
> ~God

are yours. Stand firm in God's anointing and calling for you, and then act in agreement to God's directives. Get counsel from more-seasoned Christian saints and apply it to your situation with a blanket of humility. Completely cover everything with prayer. Confirm your actions are in accordance with the Bible. And lastly, remember, just like with David, God goes before you into your battle with his victory banner of Jehovahnissi blazing.

One day my son and I rode our bicycles to school. As he dropped off his bike at the bike rack, I noticed one of his six-year-old classmates had a new mini bike. I wondered if this child knew the power he had access to. As I prayed for this child's safety, I heard the Lord say,

> "Nor do you or any of my children understand the power that undergirds you. If you did, you would never walk in fear or unbelief, or experience anxiety. You do not comprehend the power in which you pray to, or the one who paid such a high price for you. If you did, you would be living victoriously, focusing only on your God."

Although those words stung, I received the rebuke. It's true. How many of us walk in that level of confidence in our God? I know I don't and my faith wavers, especially during my trials. I believe the Lord would speak to those of us who are facing insurmountable, larger-than-life, Goliath-sized trials and remind us…

Know Who Fights for You

Lift your gaze, my child. Focus on me. Remember, no weapon formed against you shall prosper. I, *your God*, your *great Jehovahnissi*, go before you. Remember, *you* carry my victory banner in front of you. It waves before you in your battle declaring my ultimate victory over your enemies.

My divine will prevails, not the enemy's, for I AM God.

And even your presumed failures or seemingly supposed defeats, I will use for my good and for my glory. I AM *that big of a God.*

Be obedient to my leading, my child. Just watch what my sovereign hand will accomplish with you out of the way, trying to control everything with feeble human hands and powerless mortal armor instead of being on your knees praying in complete faith and submission to your God.

Know your God. Know who goes before you. Know the power of the banner of *Jehovahnissi* that waves before you in battle. *Do not doubt your God.*

For I have given you the courage to step out in faith toward your battle line, to pull out *your* sling and obey me in absolute faith.

You have heard the angry, bitter, jealous words from your fearful family and friends who are single-focused on unbelief and the apparently inescapable pain they sadly believe will be the only outcome of your trial.

You see their hearts; their focus is only on the seeming insurmountable mountain, not on *me*, the *Great* I AM.

They are so terrified of change, they desperately claw at you to keep you next to them where they think you should reside and be content, as they seemingly are.

For your obedience is too painfully convicting of their own shortcomings and past disobedience. My light from your obedience shines too brightly on them, exposing their lack of repentance for their sins and lack of faith.

They are in bondage.

I desire for them to *repent*, turn from their *sins*, and be *single-focused* on me.

Pray for them. Intercede for them. For I see you, I hear your prayers.

Their fear has blinded them, eclipsed their vision of me, the unchangeable, omnipotent, omniscient, omnipresent, transcendent, and miraculous God who loves them enough to send my one and only Son to live a perfect life, then die in complete obedience to me in full payment for their sins. This is so that they will have the opportunity to turn from their sins and place their faith in my Son.

In doing so, they will then be covered by the blood of Jesus Christ, washed clean, and therefore saved from my wrath.

For I alone have allowed this battle to come upon you, to grow you, to increase your faith in me, to draw you closer to me, your sovereign, loving God.

Lift your gaze, my child. Become single-focused on me, your God.

Your battle is not yours, but it is mine.

For I fight for you. You need only to be still.

Quiet your heart, trust in me, watch my sovereign hand at work, allow me to go ahead of you with my banner, for I AM your Jehovahnissi. I AM your *Great* I AM. I AM your Yahweh. I AM your God without borders. For I will never abandon you.

No weapon formed against you shall prosper.

Remember, I AM the God of all flesh. *Is there anything too hard for me?* Even you will be amazed at my sovereign hand at work. I alone fight for you.

Continue in your supplication, adoration, worship, and prayer toward me. *Do not focus on your enemy.* Do not even entertain his words, for he is the father of all lies. Do not let your sights be upon him. Do not let your vision be eclipsed by your enemy's seemingly massiveness.

He is not even a mere flea compared to me, your God!

Focus on me. *Remember who fights for you*!

I will never depart from you nor disown you.

I AM your God.

Some of you reading this are embroiled in combat, and the thought of God going before you is too much to grasp. Your response is anything but trusting in God. You can't seem to grab ahold of anything secure, as life is just madly swirling around you.

Others may have received life-altering battle wounds from your trial. You may be angry with God. He did something you didn't like or took something or someone you loved, and you are in bondage to your fear and anger. You are lost in the valley of death. You might also be overcome by darkness, sadness, and depression. When it completely overtakes you, you can't even begin to see your God. Or your anger might be seeping out at the most inopportune moments, and you are struggling to keep your head above the deep waters of your trial.

Then there are some of you who have been through the war and have seen God work miraculously. You are now experiencing the amazing bountiful fruit God has created in your life through your trial and are satisfied. But God is not done with you yet. He wants to continue to use you in new ways, in new pastures, and you are fighting these new giftings he is developing in you.

And lastly, some of you have tasted and seen that God is good, and like the young King David, you are willing and ready for the next trial or battle, knowing your God goes before you.

Whatever camp you are in, this is my prayer for you …

Dear God,

Draw near to my friends who are reading this right now. Pour out your Spirit into them. Where there is doubt, fill them with your courage. Where there is lack of faith in your awesomeness, *lift their gaze* to you.

Where there is confusion over your divine will for their life, show them your plan for them in your Word, the Holy Bible. Where their seemingly well-meaning loved ones have spoken out against them as they walk in obedience to your calling, give them a stronger resoluteness and peace that transcends all understanding to follow your will with an unwavering single-focused, God-centered vision.

Regardless of where they are at, pour out your peace upon them. Give them your joy during their struggle. Help them remember who fights for them.

Lift their gaze to you, oh God!

Allow them to see and experience a greater vision of you, Lord. Show them how BIG you really are and how small their trials are compared to you a holy, perfect, omniscient, omnipresent, omnipotent, transcendent, and unchangeable God.

Help them walk in obedience to your sovereign will and calling on their life despite the opposition of their loved ones.

Lift their gaze. Fight for them, oh King! Increase their faith, oh mighty God!

Amaze them! *Lift the scales of unbelief from their eyes.* Fix their gaze on you, oh Lord. For you are their God. You are the Great I AM.

You are their Jehovahnissi. You fight for them. Your banner goes ahead of them. Remove the fear and spiritual paralysis in their lives.

Bless them with your joy despite their trials. Help them, oh King.

Draw near to them. Lift their gaze so it is solely focused on *you*, the Great I AM.

Again, amaze them, oh GOD!

In Jesus' precious name I pray.

Amen!

APPLICATION QUESTIONS

Getting to the Heart of It

1. Have you ever faced or are you currently facing a situation that seems impossible? Describe.

2. How have you seen the faithfulness of God in the past when it initially seemed that you were destined to fail?

3. What did you learn from the experience, and how did it change you?

4. Have you ever had to walk in obedience to God's leading when your well-meaning family and/or friends tried to discourage you? If so, describe.

5. How have you tried to wear another person's armor even though God has called you to something different?

6. How does it comfort you knowing that the God who created the universe—who is all-powerful, all-knowing, all-present, without time, unchangeable, without sin, the God of miracles, your refuge and strength—is already ahead of you, fighting your battles for you?

"Every good and perfect gift is from above, coming down from the *Father of the heavenly lights, who does not change like shifting shadows.*

~ JAMES 1:17 NIV *emphasis mine*

1. Before presenting your prayer requests to God, remind yourself of whom you are praying to. List five new attributes of God you haven't listed yet.

   1 ______
   2 ______
   3 ______
   4 ______
   5 ______

2. Then list at least five additional blessings (ones you haven't listed before) in your life that you are grateful for.

   1 ______
   2 ______
   3 ______
   4 ______
   5 ______

   ______

3. List your prayer requests.

4. Write down anything else the Lord is speaking to your heart.

5. Finally, close by praising God in advance for whatever the outcome.

CHAPTER TEN

The Whole Armor of God

Finally, be strong in the Lord and in the strength of his might. *Put on the whole armor of God, that you may be able to stand against the schemes of the devil.* For we do not wrestle against flesh and blood, but against the rulers, against the authorities, against the cosmic powers over this present darkness, against the spiritual forces of evil in the heavenly places. Therefore take up *the whole armor of God, that you may be able to withstand in the evil day, and having done all, to stand firm.* Stand therefore, having fastened on the belt of truth, and having put on the breastplate of righteousness, and, as shoes for your feet, having put on the readiness given by the gospel of peace. In all circumstances take up the shield of faith, with which you can extinguish all the flaming darts of the evil one; and take the helmet of salvation, and the sword of the Spirit, which is the word of God, praying at all times in the Spirit, with all prayer and supplication. *To that end keep alert with all perseverance, making supplication for all the saints.*

~ EPHESIANS 6:10–18 *emphasis mine*

"PLEASE PRAY FOR me," I said to one of my friends as we started our prayer walk. The sky was a beautiful shade of light blue, contrasting the soft white cloud lines.

"Why? What's up?" She looked at me with concerned eyes.

"I'm scheduled to go on a mission trip to Uganda this month, and it seems like the enemy is throwing everything at me, including the kitchen sink," I blurted out.

"What's going on?"

Her eyes got wider and wider with each incident I shared with her. "Kim, *this* is what I saw in that vision I told you about months ago!" she interrupted.

I had no idea what she was talking about. "What? I don't remember. Tell me again."

"You *don't* remember?" she repeated, rolling her eyes.

I shook my head in disagreement, squinting into the sun as I again searched the deep recesses of my memory.

Another eye roll. Her hand motions got more animated with each word. "I told you I saw you going into a really dark place—a spiritually dark place—that was without God. But God had you and the people you were with in a bubble of protection. It was like he went before you, cleared the path, protected you while you were there, and then safely brought you and your team out of there and back home." She stared at me with her huge brown eyes, palms facing upward in finality.

"Oh, *that's* what you were referring to," I mumbled.

"Yes!"

"Well, that's encouraging. So the enemy already knows all the good that will come from this trip and he's out to thwart me," I said with a smirk.

"And the great news is that God is bigger than the enemy," she exclaimed. "He's going ahead of you and is covering you completely. He's got this!"

I stopped in my tracks. "Wow. He's covering me with his armor, like in Ephesians!" We had been studying the armor of God in my small group at church.

"Exactly!"

We chatted and finished our prayer walk, praising God in advance for what he was and is going to do in both of our lives.

My trip to Uganda was life-altering in so many ways. It was truly a place of great beauty and amazing people coupled with profound spiritual darkness and hatred because of my skin color. But the darker the place, the brighter the light. My time there brought so many revelations of God's care and his armor surrounding me. From the blooming acacia trees, to not having clean running water or adequate sewage, to seeing the women being treated like servants, I felt like I was transported back to biblical times. It comforted me that no matter where we are, we are never too far away from the protective hand of God. He is our shield and buckler (Psalm 35:2), a very present help in times of trouble (Psalm 46:1). He is our great God, the Great I AM, our Jehovah, our Yahweh.

God also makes it apparent in Ephesians that we don't grapple against other humans (as sometimes we think we do), but instead, we wrestle against spiritual forces that are not of God.

A quote by Corrie ten Boom always convicts me of how ridiculous it is to doubt God during our difficult times: "When a train goes through a tunnel and it gets dark, you don't throw away the ticket and jump off. You sit still and trust the engineer."[1] We need to focus on God, not the darkness, just like David did with Goliath. And God gives us just the thing we need to do that. Every day, like other giants in the faith, our second response to a trial (after remembering who

> "We must resolve by God's grace, not to yield to Satan. Resist him, and he will flee. If we give way, he will get ground. If we distrust either our cause, or our Leader, or our armour, we give him advantage."
> ~ MATTHEW HENRY

goes before us) is to put on the *entire* armor of God. We can't forget even one piece.

We need to daily prepare ourselves like warriors going into battle, by choosing the correct weapons for combat. "For the weapons of our warfare are not of the flesh but have divine power to destroy strongholds" (2 Corinthians 10:4). The battleground is the present day amid a seemingly chaotic fallen world. God is still sovereign over our lives, despite the attacks from the enemy. Looking more closely at the arsenal at our disposal in Ephesians 6:10–18, we see God's comprehensive and impenetrable protection over us.

Before putting on the armor, we need to understand the difference between our responsibility and God's. God creates and bestows upon us the armor; it is our duty to wear it for the *entire* battle, despite how weary we feel.[2] For the enemy has a myriad of ways to tempt us to denigrate our God.[3] It is our role to trust our armor and our God. Matthew Henry states in his commentary:

> We must resolve by God's grace, not to yield to Satan. Resist him, and he will flee. If we give way, he will get ground. If we distrust either our cause, or our Leader, or our armour, we give him advantage.[4]

1. The Belt of Truth

First and foremost, we are to put on the belt of truth. The width of a Roman soldier's belt was very thick. It was used to hold their sword and as a girdle to strengthen and uphold the core.[5] The belt is listed first, because like *truth*, it is the most important part—it holds everything together. Even Jesus attested to the importance of undergirding oneself in truth when he responded to Pontius Pilate, who was about to authorize the gruesome torture of Truth in the flesh:

> "For this purpose I was born and for this purpose I have come into the world—to bear witness to the truth. Everyone who is of the truth listens to my voice." (John 18:37)

Pilate then ignorantly asked, "What is truth?" (John 18:38). He was blind to the Truth. He was staring at Truth, Jesus Christ, God incarnate, in the face.

Jesus, our High Priest, interceded to God on our behalf, when he prayed, "Sanctify them in the truth; your word is truth" (John 17:17). We all need the solid, unmovable truth from Jesus Christ, especially when the due north of our moral compass fluctuates erratically, depending on what's currently trending in our society. In our culture, truth is based on popularity ratings, media coverage, and the loudest voices blasting through our televisions, computers, and smartphones. Christ is Truth. And he, being Truth, is only revealed in his Word, the Holy Bible.

2. The Breastplate of Righteousness

Every day, we have a choice of what we are going to put on. Are we putting on righteousness over our heart? Are we going to walk in a manner worthy of our calling as a servant of God? Or are we going to put on unrighteousness? Will we selfishly indulge in actions God considers sinful and deeds that are hurtful to others? Are we going to daily receive Christ's imputed righteousness, which is readily available to all who are in Christ Jesus?

We have a choice. And we desperately need the grace of God to walk in a manner worthy of our calling. We cannot do it by our own strength. It's only through our faith in Jesus that we can turn from unrighteousness. Jesus Christ lived a perfect, sinless, and righteous life. And because of our faith in him as our personal Savior and the complete work on the cross, his righteousness is credited to us. The indispensable breastplate of righteousness of our Lord Jesus absorbs the entirety of God's divine wrath and destroys the arrows of the enemy.[6]

The indispensable breastplate of righteousness of our Lord Jesus absorbs the entirety of God's divine wrath and destroys the arrows of the enemy.

Martin Luther once likened our sinful nature to a dunghill and the righteousness of Christ as a thick blanket of freshly fallen snow on top of it. The huge manure pile is no longer a disgusting, revolting, and foul-smelling hill, but now is a beautiful, glistening, purified, and spotless mound of Christ's righteousness imputed on us.[7] Understanding and accepting that Christ's pure and sinless covering is all God sees when he looks at us gives the enemy no foothold in our life for judgment and denunciation. We are immersed in the righteousness of Christ. Therefore, *there is no condemnation for those in Christ Jesus* (Romans 8:1).

3. The Gospel of Peace

After the breastplate of righteousness, we need to place the readiness of the gospel of peace as shoes for our feet. Another translation for the word *gospel* is "good news." If we are daily walking in the knowledge of the good news of Christ's death for us, we can be at peace and reconciled with a holy and perfect God. The power and the peace that transcends all understanding should be palatable with every one of our footsteps.

Roman soldiers wore greaves, iron or bronze shin protectors, to protect them in battle as well as from the wounds of the sharp and thorny terrain.[8] As Christians, our protections for our legs are not metal; rather, they are a "peaceful and benevolent temper"[9] of the gospel that shields us from the enemy and unknown territory.

They also had long spikes or nails protruding downward from the soles of their battle shoes to secure each step so that they wouldn't be forced backward in the battle.[10] Their footing would then be firm and anchored, therefore preventing the enemy to gain not an inch during the battle.

The power and the peace that transcends all understanding should be palatable with every one of our footsteps.

It is the same for us. The spikes extending from our shoes must be steeped in the gospel of peace. Each time we seek peace with someone we sin against or who sinned against us, we impart the gospel. It embeds us more deeply in Christ. Every confident step of the saint walking firmly in the shoes of the gospel of peace strips the enemy of his already weakening power.

4. The Shield of Faith

Make no mistake—the evil one expertly throws painful flaming darts to our weakest areas. Matthew Henry's biblical commentary attests that our faith is everything during our battle: "Faith, as relying on unseen objects, receiving Christ and the benefits of redemption, and so deriving grace from him, is like a shield, a defense (in) every way."[11]

Whatever we have not given over to God to be used as his and his alone, Satan *will* use to remove your focus from God. He *will* try to steal your joy. It is his goal to completely debilitate you and paralyze you with fear and anguish. Whether employing money, children, fame, vanity, home, business, health, or even the church, Satan will attack these areas with lies, deceptions, dread, anxieties, and other wicked ploys to remove your focus from God.

How are we to extinguish the flaming darts of the evil one? Our best offense is to have an unwavering defense. And God has provided one for us—our shield of faith, the Word of God. Our most mighty weapon of defense against the onslaught of the enemy's fire is our faith in our all-powerful, all-knowing, all-present, faithful, and holy God.

> Anyone or anything that causes you to doubt God's goodness, love, or care of you is from the enemy. *Period.*

We need to be single-focused on God in faith. We will not prevail in talking, arguing, debating, or reasoning with sin or Satan. Eve found that out firsthand in the garden. By dialoguing with Satan, she unknowingly exposed herself and her husband to his skilled distortion of the Word of God. Our adversary enabled her to doubt God's love, faithfulness, and provision. He challenged Eve's pride with cunning manipulation. She attempted in her own strength and intelligence to refute the serpent. And then his pièce de résistance: he tauntingly dangled something we all long for, to be like God.

> "You will not surely die. For God knows that when you eat of it your eyes will be opened, and *you will*

> *be like God, knowing good and evil.*" (Genesis 3:4–5 emphasis mine)

Anyone or anything that causes you to doubt God's goodness, love, or care of you is from the enemy. *Period.* Jesus even encountered this among his own disciples, when he was preparing them that he would suffer, be killed, and then raised from the dead in three days when he returned to Jerusalem (Matthew 16:21). Peter, like most of us, frequently speaking before thinking, responded, "'Far be it from you, Lord! This shall never happen to you'" (Matthew 16:22 NIV). Jesus rebuked Peter:

> "Get behind me, Satan! You are a stumbling block to me; you do not have in mind the concerns of God, but merely human concerns." (Matthew 16:23 NIV).

If Jesus was completely fixated on the cross and had to die for us on it, then how much more should we be single-focused on the cross and what was done for us on it?

It wasn't nails that held Jesus to the cross, for he could have commanded legions of angels to come down to rescue him (Matthew 26:53). It was Jesus Christ's *love* for us—sinners, enemies of God—that held him there. He paid the complete payment for our sins. Our *faith* in Jesus Christ and the love he displayed for us on that cross is how we take up the shield of faith and nullify the trifling attacks of the enemy. We will

If Jesus was completely fixated on the cross and had to die for us on it, then how much more should we be single-focused on the cross and what was done for us on it?

then see that all things are under God's sovereign hand and control. We need to boldly use our shield of faith in unwavering confidence in our God, who valiantly fights for us.

5. The Helmet of Salvation

The head is the most important part of our body. That is why we have helmet laws for motorcyclists and bicyclists. A cranium injury affects the whole body, as does a spiritual injury to the brain.

The enemy's favorite battleground where he can take the greatest advantage of unsuspecting followers of Jesus Christ is our mind. When we allow him to take our focus off God and put it onto our battle, he completely incapacitates us. Our trial gets bigger than our God. Satan fills our mind with fear, uncertainty, and doubt. We then forget our God. This is his most effective and most-used weapon.

We, like soldiers in battle, must protect our mind. We do so by using the helmet of the promise of eternal salvation. As followers of Christ, we are promised eternal life with God, Jesus Christ, and the Holy Spirit. We will *never* experience an eternity of damnation. Remembering and speaking the truth that we are covered by the blood of Jesus completely eradicates the power of the enemy. *Jesus saves.* And Jesus has saved those who trust in him for their salvation. *Our greatest need has already been met on that cross!* We need to put on the helmet of salvation daily.

The truth that we are covered by the blood of Jesus completely eradicates the power of the enemy. *Jesus saves.*

6. The Sword of the Spirit

The Word of God, the sword of the Spirit, is the only offensive weapon we wear. It is our double-edged short blade, like a dagger,[12] and it is comparable to the one Peter used to cut off Malchus's ear in the garden of Gethsemane (John 18:10). It's also a powerful divisive tool separating good and evil:

> For the word of God is living and active, sharper than *any two-edged sword*, piercing to the division of soul and of spirit, of joints and of marrow, and discerning the thoughts and intentions of the heart. (Hebrews 4:12 emphasis mine)

This same weapon can also be an instrument of judgment by a magistrate or judge to invoke death by the sword:[13]

> Who shall separate us from the love of Christ? Shall tribulation, or distress, or persecution, or famine, or nakedness, or danger, or *sword*? (Romans 8:35 emphasis mine).

We are to hold steady to this weapon of the Word of God and guard our hearts and minds with it in Christ Jesus. This is the same blade the Son of God used when he was tempted by the enemy as he fasted for forty days and nights in the wilderness. Satan tempted to fulfill Jesus' immediate physical needs of hunger, and attacked Jesus' divinity by putting him to the test and then finally with worldly power as Satan promised to give Jesus all the kingdoms of the world if he just bowed down and worshiped just him (Matthew 4:1–11).

Each time he was tested, Jesus did not respond like Adam with silence or like Eve with counter arguments and an ensuing debate. Rather, Jesus simply responded with his greatest weapon, the Word of God. Dumbfounded and beaten, Satan departed, and angels ministered to the weary Jesus (Matthew 4:11).

> We are to hold steady to this weapon of the Word of God and guard our hearts and minds with it in Christ Jesus.

If the Son of God needed the dagger of Scripture to defend himself against the onslaught of the enemy during his trial, how much do we need to commit Scripture to memory for our battles? It is *our* responsibility to master our recall of Scripture, especially verses that give us hope and peace.

If we are struggling to memorize Scripture, we have a partner to assist us. Praying to the Holy Spirit, our Helper (John 14:26), gives us access to the most powerful force in nature, our Creator. God states that he is the "Lord, the God of all flesh. Is anything too hard for me?" (Jeremiah 32:27)

As we select our battle Scriptures and plaster them everywhere—in our car, on our refrigerator, on our computer, in our office, on our bathroom mirror, etc.—we give ourselves an undeniable stronghold against the enemy.

Here are a few of my favorites. Read them aloud for the full effect:

> And we know that for those who love God, all things work together for good, for those who are called according to his purpose. (Romans 8:28)
>
> What then shall we say to these things? If God is for us, who can be against us? (Romans 8:31)

He who did not spare his own Son but gave him up for us all, how will he not also with him graciously give us all things? (Romans 8:32)

For I know the plans I have for you, declares the Lord, plans for welfare and not for evil, to give you a future and a hope. (Jeremiah 29:11)

Then you will call upon me and come and pray to me, and I will hear you. (Jeremiah 29:12)

Then he said to me, "This is the word of the Lord to Zerubbabel: Not by might, nor by power, but by my Spirit, says the Lord of hosts." (Zechariah 4:6)

The Lord your God is he who goes with you to fight for you against your enemies, to give you the victory. (Deuteronomy 20:4)

"Be still, and know that I am God. I will be exalted among the nations, I will be exalted in the earth!" (Psalm 46:10)

I can do all things through him who strengthens me. (Philippians 4:13)

Little children, you are from God and have overcome them, for he who is in you is greater than he who is in the world. (1 John 4:4)

"For nothing will be impossible with God." (Luke 1:37)

The Word of God has the power to render the enemy powerless; it pronounces and declares his impending judgment (Revelation 11). And the good news is that we have unlimited access to wielding this sword of the Word of God in our battles.

7. Praying at All Times in the Spirit with Supplication

Oh, the power of prayer! If we really understood the depth and magnitude of the power we have access to through our prayers, we could transform the entire world! Jesus, the Son of God, sets the example for us. He frequently spent time away from the masses and his beloved disciples to pray. If Jesus needed prayer and solitude with God, the Father, then how much more do we, mere mortals, need to be praying always?

Jesus even instructed his disciples how to pray:

> "Our Father in heaven, hallowed be your name. Your kingdom come, your will be done, on earth as it is in heaven. Give us this day our daily bread, and forgive us our debts, as we also have forgiven our debtors. And lead us not into temptation, but deliver us from evil." (Matthew 6:9–13)

Oh, the power of prayer! If we really understood the depth and magnitude of the power we have access to through our prayers, we could transform the entire world!

How, then, do we pray in the Spirit? Certain people believe that praying in the Spirit is only praying in tongues. Although some do have the gift of tongues, not everyone does. And if we all don't have this gift, are the people who don't have this gift supposed to *not* pray in the Spirit? We should pray that the Holy Spirit would direct our prayers and that they would be in accordance to God's divine will. This resonates in God's promise to us:

> This is the confidence that we have toward him, that if we ask anything according to his will he hears us. And if we know that he hears us in whatever we ask, we know that we have the requests that we have asked of him. (1 John 5:14–15)

Praying Scripture back to God is our most powerful weapon. Never underestimate the power of praying Scripture over another person, yourself, or an event. By reciting God's promises in complete faith with humble supplication, a pure heart, and without hypocrisy,[14] we are praying in the Spirit. We have confidence that we are only able to approach the throne of a holy God and present our requests to him because of his grace through our faith in his Son. Since you have repented from your sins and have trusted in Jesus as your personal Savior, you now have the Holy Spirit inside you (Acts 2:38) and have access to the throne room and direct access to God.

Praying Scripture back to God is our most powerful weapon.

Prayer is the fastener that keeps all our Christian armor binded together.[15] Without it, everything just falls off. Matthew Henry explains in his Bible commentary that despite any discouragements, by the grace of God:

> We must pray with all kinds of prayer, public, private, and secret; social and solitary; solemn and sudden:

> with all the parts of prayer; confession of sin, petition for mercy, and thanksgiving for favors received.[16]

Praying not just for us and our loved ones; praying also for those who sin against us (Luke 6:28). We all desperately need prayer, and this is our responsibility and joy as Christians.

8. Keeping Alert with All Perseverance

Trials and battles with the enemy can make us weary. We need to persevere and "be alert and of sober mind. Your enemy the devil prowls around like a roaring lion looking for someone to devour" (1 Peter 5:8 NIV). If you are immersed in heavy enemy fire, *look up.*

If you are immersed in heavy enemy fire, *look up.*

Just like the army's ground forces, when they are immersed in heavy fire, they call for close air support. They continue to fight, yet still look skyward in anticipation for their protection—as should we. We need to lift our gaze to our God and pray for a fresh indwelling of the Holy Spirit so that we can stay the course. We are to remain steadfast; hold firm to the power, might, and sovereignty of our God; and remember how limited the power of the enemy is compared to God. We are a coveted child of God—the enemy is not.

9. Make Supplications for All the Saints

Independence is another great lie of the enemy. We are called to surround ourselves with other believers for so many reasons. When one is weak in faith, the other is strong. We cannot fight this battle alone. We need to be united in the gospel, worship, and prayer. When we are, we increase exponentially in power, strength, and might against the enemy.

> **We have immense, untapped power in prayer.**

Someone once said that Christians are like embers from a fire. If you separate an individual ember from the fire, it becomes dark, loses its strength, and eventually extinguishes. Consequentially, if you place the ember back in the blazing fire, the ember will reignite and increase in heat and power. Know that the enemy knows that truth and will use your trial to try to separate you from other believers. Even in nature, wolves look for the sheep who have wandered away from the flock and are now vulnerable; those are the ones they attack. We have immense, untapped power in prayer:

> Therefore confess your sins to each other and pray for each other so that you may be healed. The prayer of a righteous person is powerful and effective. (James 5:16 NIV)

God hears our prayers and answers us in his perfect timing. He is never early, and he is never late. As those who have placed our faith in Jesus Christ, it is our calling to go before the throne of grace in supplication for all the saints who are suffering and in need of prayer.

10. Putting It All Together

As one of the most helpful and uplifting exercises of faith, the Lord had me enter my name in the Scripture in Ephesians 6:10–18 and it was life changing. I understood what my responsibility was during a period of suffering and what was not. I was not supposed to be in denial of the turmoil around me, sucking my spiritual thumb and waiting on God to move. I needed to *pray*, remember *who* I was fighting *against*, understand *who* was fighting *for* me, and *affix* my *gaze* on *my problem-solver*, not my *problems*.

I encourage—no, I implore you—to do the same. Comprehend the power you pray to. Know your God. You pray to the God of all creation—an omnipotent, omnipresent, omniscient, transcendent, amazing, awesome, holy, and righteous God. Digest and act on the authority who backs you during your trial.

I needed to pray, remember who I was fighting against, understand who was fighting for me, and affix my gaze on my problem-solver, not my problems.

Discern your enemy, recognize his schemes, and understand that your enemy is subject to the authority and sovereignty of God. Accept that your enemy is powerless against the blood of Jesus, which covers *all* who have repented, turned from their sins, and believe in Jesus Christ as their personal Savior. Fathom the depth of who fights for you. Know *who* goes ahead of you in battle. And most of all, master your role as a warrior. Receive comfort that when someone sins against you, you are not contending against them but against your common enemy.

If Jesus Christ, God in the flesh, needed the whole armor of God just to stand firm against the devil, then how much more do we need it? Indulge yourself and *read out loud* Ephesians 6:10–18 (next page) with your name in the blanks. I pray this touches you deeply, pours down into your soul like fresh wind, and refreshes you with the spiritual deluge that only the Holy Spirit could provide.

The Whole Armor of God Prayer

Finally, ______________ is strong in the Lord, in the strength of his/her might. ____________ puts on the whole armor of God, so that ____________ is able to stand against the schemes of the devil. __________ does not wrestle against flesh and blood, but against rulers, against the authorities, against the cosmic powers over this present darkness, against the spiritual forces of evil in the heavenly places.

Therefore, __________________ takes up the whole armor of God, so that ________________ is able to withstand in the evil day, and having done all, to stand firm. ______________ therefore stands, having fastened on the belt of truth, and having put on the breastplate of righteousness and _____________ puts on the readiness given by the gospel of peace as shoes for _____________ 's feet. In all circumstances, ______________ takes up the shield of faith, with which ______________ extinguishes all the flaming darts of the evil one; and _______________ takes the helmet of salvation, and the sword of the Spirit, which is the Word of God, praying at all times in the Spirit, with all prayer and supplication. _______________ to that end

> keeps alert with all perseverance, making supplications for all the saints. (Ephesians 6:10–18 with personalization).

Look closely at each of those verses, which is now your very own prayer. Notice there is no armor for the back—no protection for those who turn and flee from the enemy and leave the faith. The armor is only for those who stand firm in the Lord. Again, we must not waver in our focus and trust of God, our cause, our Savior, or our armor, lest we give our enemy the slightest unneeded advantage.[15]

We must comprehend that God is allowing this tribulation—this battle—to shape us, to mold us, to humble us, and to fashion us into a more accurate image of his Son. Rest in the truth of your refinement with the assurance that God works all things out for good and his glory.

Rest in the truth of your refinement with the assurance that God works all things out for good and his glory.

The Lord of hosts commands all the armies of angels, orders our steps, and changes our hearts. I believe the sovereign God of the universe would open his arms and welcome you into his embrace with…

The Whole Armor of God

Breathe, my child. You are too focused on the schemes of the enemy, not on me. I have given you everything you need to defend yourself: the belt of truth, breastplate of righteousness, shield of faith, helmet of salvation, sword of the Spirit, and, most importantly, prayer in the Spirit.

You are at your strongest on your knees, covered in my love. For I hear your prayers. Pray for me to change *you* first, not the situation.

I am doing a good work in you through this trial. Trust me.

You are mine. I have paid a great price for you. I will never cast you away.

I have entire armies of angels at my disposal, yet I choose this battle specifically to strengthen you and force you to look to me, your Creator in worship, despite the pain and affliction you are experiencing. You are my beloved child.

Battles strengthen warriors.

You are my prayer warrior and are covered by my blood.

I am yours and you are mine.

Just praise me in advance.

I have this.

Some of you reading this now are embroiled in combat. For some of you, your heart aches for a loved one who is walking through a season of trials. Maybe some of you are just coasting as you have been given a temporary reprieve. And some of you might be in a season of blessings. Wherever God has you, this is my prayer for you …

Dear God,

I pray for my friends, your chosen vessels, who are reading this now. I pray your Holy Spirit would help them put on the whole armor of God, having done all to stand against the attacks of the enemy.

I pray for a bigger vision of who you are, your power, might, and holiness. Let them see exactly *who* they are praying to. Reveal *yourself* to them. Show them your Shekinah glory, the very glory that filled the entire temple of God when King Solomon dedicated it. Show them that same power is in them through their faith in Christ Jesus. Fill them with your Holy Spirit.

Help them *lift their gaze* and bless them. Help them put on the belt of truth so that all who see them will behold the truth of Christ in them. Anchor on them the breastplate of righteousness that is available to all believers in Christ Jesus. Bless them with the infallible shield of faith that extinguishes the flaming darts of the evil one.

Place on their heads the helmet of salvation so that they know beyond a shadow of a doubt, they are saved by Christ Jesus. Let them know that by their faith in their Savior, their greatest need of being rescued from an eternity in hell has already been met.

Impart on them the flaming sword of the Spirit, steeping them deeply in Scripture, so their only response to their trials is to repeat the Word of God, which is living and active in them, sharper than any two-edged sword, breaking the power of sin and the enemy over their lives.

Enable them to easily memorize Scripture, supernaturally applying it to their lives in new and unique ways so that it is crystal clear they are separate from the world, set apart as your chosen vessel, only for your good work.

Help them pray always in the Spirit in humility, in accordance to your divine will. Have them earnestly seek your divine will for their lives. Help them joyfully live within the boundaries you have set in pleasant places over their lives.

Oh Lord, empower them to keep alert, to not grow weary, to persevere despite the length or severity of their battle. Pour out your desire in them to forgive quickly, cry out to you on other saints' behalf, and passionately intercede for all the saints.

Draw those who have walked away from your church back to your church to increase in your light, power, and steadfastness. Bless them, Father, in all things, so that they can stand firmly in you, their God, as you fight for them. Enlarge their faith in you. Allow them to see what a BIG and amazing God you really are.

Bless them, oh King. Do an amazing work in them. Increase in them.

Have them decrease, trusting completely in you.

In Jesus' precious name, I pray.

Amen.

APPLICATION QUESTIONS

Getting to the Heart of It

1. Describe a time or situation when you felt the attack of the enemy. How did you overcome?

2. Has God ever used you to show the gospel of peace in times when you were sinned against and wanted to retaliate but instead extended peace? Describe the situation and outcome.

3. Give an example of when you have chosen to walk in righteousness instead of unrighteousness? Describe the results.

4. Describe a time when you walked in unrighteousness and the outcome of your decision.

5. Did you repent of your unrighteousness and leave it at the cross, knowing it was paid in full by Christ's complete work on the cross? If not, why?

6. How does knowing that even Jesus used memorized Scripture to combat the attack of the enemy comfort you? What new Scripture verses will you memorize?

Be joyful in *hope*, patient in *affliction*, faithful in *prayer*.

~ Romans 12:12 NIV *emphasis mine*

1. Before presenting your prayer requests to God, remind yourself of who God is. List five of God's attributes (such as all-powerful, all-present, all-knowing, holy, without the confines of time, almighty, majestic, beautiful, etc.).

   1 ______________________________
   2 ______________________________
   3 ______________________________
   4 ______________________________
   5 ______________________________

2. Then list at least five blessings (different ones from previous chapters) in your life that you are grateful for.

   1 ______________________________
   2 ______________________________
   3 ______________________________
   4 ______________________________
   5 ______________________________
   ____

3. List your prayer requests.

4. Write down anything else the Lord is speaking to your heart.

5. Finally, close by praising God to remind yourself of what an awesome God he is. And praise him in advance for whatever the outcome.

CHAPTER ELEVEN

Down to the Dregs

Even if I am to be poured out as a drink offering upon the sacrificial offering of your faith, *I am glad and rejoice with you all.*

~ PHILIPPIANS 2:17 *emphasis mine*

Its drink offering shall be a quarter of a hin for each lamb. In the Holy place you shall pour out a drink offering of strong drink to the Lord.

~ NUMBERS 28:7

Again, for the second time, he went away and prayed, *"My Father, if this cannot pass unless I drink it, your will be done."*

~ MATTHEW 26:42 *emphasis mine*

I DIDN'T WANT TO do it. Not even a little bit. Nope, I was done.

My legs ached. Every joint in my feet and toes seemed to scream with each step. My lower back was tighter than a rubber band ready to snap. I ached all over and was beyond tired.

I groaned as I pulled my car into my friend's driveway. It was the day of our twenty-two-mile training run for our marathon in a few weeks. It would be my second marathon, her first. Months ago, I had promised to help her train for it. And as her trainer, motivator, and coach, I didn't want to move any of my muscles, let alone go for an extended run.

I smiled as she got into the car. Of course, I was glad to see her and spend time with her, just not while running in the hot sun.

She sighed as she sat down. I saw the exhaustion in her face. The intense training schedule was getting to us both. Even though I had been through this season once before and I knew this was the hard part of marathon training, it didn't make these long runs any easier.

This was the time during marathon training that everything hurt. The combination of our high weekly miles and the long weekend runs were painfully breaking down our muscles, yet in doing so making us physically stronger. We were also triumphing over the mental anguish of pushing through our pain despite how we felt.

I hated this part.

"So how are you doing?" I asked with a knowing nod.

She exploded in frustration as she poured out a detailed itemization of her pain and dread for our run.

Laughing in agreement with her transparency, I responded with a hearty, "I hear you!"

She looked at me like I had lost my running marbles. For the past several months during our training, I had always been so positive and encouraging. This was the first time she heard me voice any objections.

"No, really. I'm right there with you!" I exclaimed. "I just want to go back to bed. I am so unbelievably tired. I told myself this morning, *I already ran a marathon, I'm good. I don't need to run forty miles a week anymore. I'm too old for this!*"

She looked at me with her head canted and said, "You know, you don't have to do it with me. I'll be okay. Somehow, I'll run this marathon. Please feel released."

Silence.

Then a switch flipped in my heart as I burst out in laughter. I slapped the steering wheel as I continued to drive us to the exercise path. "No, this is normal. This is the hard part of the training. It's the mental game. We *are* going to run today, no matter how we *feel*. We *are* going to run to prepare our bodies and our mental state for this marathon in a few weeks, all by the grace of God."

"Are you sure?" she asked.

With firm resolve that surprised even me, I said, "Yes, absolutely. I made a commitment to you and this race. And despite how I or we feel, we are going to be obedient and press on. Remember, this is the dark side of marathon training. This is normal."

"That's right, you *did* say that!" she remembered, tapping one finger on her chin with a slight smile.

I pulled into the parking lot of the trail. "Okay, then. Let's do this. And let's pray to God for help. We're going to need it!"

We prayed, and despite the heat, aching legs, and weary hearts, we finished the entire twenty-two-mile training run in just over four and half hours. We also finished the subsequent grueling marathon a few weeks later.

Wanting to give up is normal, especially when you're exhausted and weary from the trial. And the thought of doing something strenuous to help someone else achieve their goal, when you are depleted, can be mentally unsettling. Pressing in to God for the strength to serve others during suffering is a true act of love. But that's the third way we are to respond to our trials.

When we're so focused on ourselves, our agony, and our trial, we miss something amazing that God is doing through us in the middle of our pain. It is in our darkest hour, with the great Jehovahnissi's banner blazing and shod in full battle gear, when the Lord gently tells us to *do* exactly what *he did*. We are to be like Jesus and humble ourselves to serve others, to become a drink offering, completely poured out for *his* service.

Jesus did just that. He did exceedingly more than my act of running another marathon to help a friend reach her goal. He drank the entire cup of God's wrath down to its dregs. He absorbed all our depravity so that for the first time in the history of creation, God could not look on his beloved Son. God had to completely reject his own Son so that we will never be abandoned.

> Pressing in to God for the strength to serve others during suffering is a true act of love.

Jesus took our punishment and paid the balance for all our sins in full. If we owed God $1 billion in debt for our sins, Jesus paid over $1 centillion (303 zeros) for us to be redeemed and reconciled with a holy God. Jesus absorbed the equivalent of a universe (2 trillion galaxies) of evil. He was poured out unequivocally as our drink offering to God. The totality of all of humankind's sins were encapsulated and funneled into one man and nailed to the cross. Jesus' single act of obedience altered the eternal trajectory for *all* those who put their hope in him as their personal Savior.

Jesus laid the unwavering foundation for how we are to respond to our trials. We are to exhibit the same humble response Jesus instructed Peter to display after he had just denied the Lord three times during Jesus' darkest hour (Matthew 14:66–72): "'Feed my lambs. . . . Tend my sheep. . . . Feed my sheep'" (John 21:15–17). All three actions require selfless love: nursing the immature, managing the exuberant, and increasing the developed.

We are to die to ourselves in our flesh, bless others during our darkest moments, and nourish those the Lord places in our lives. Just like Jesus, we are to be poured out like a drink offering. Only then in our trials will we receive the miracle of joy—as an exquisite God-wrapped and custom-made gift. It's a reward given only to those who focus on serving others during their suffering.

When we turn our myopic laser-focus *from* our difficulties *to* others, the love of Jesus is revealed. It is only through hardship's deep crevices and cracks that the light of Christ can be seen. In doing so, we can rejoice that we share in Christ's sufferings, so that we may be glad when his glory is revealed (1 Peter 4:13). Then we are bestowed the honor of the validation of Christ's suffering and are clothed in his glory. This is unveiled first to others, then ourselves, as we get to experience a sliver of eternal joy.

By humbly placing ourselves in the hand of the miracle worker, we can then be used as a redemptive instrument to bless others. Our pain is not wasted; it is used for good and to glorify God.

One of my favorite examples of this is found in a boy sitting in the middle of a sea of people in a barren land, watching Jesus speak and heal the sick. These folks and their children had been there all day in the scorching sun, soaking in the sermons from the greatest preacher who ever lived.

Envision a large stadium, with no access to food for the entire day, brimming with fifteen thousand sunburned, hungry, and starting-to-get-testy people (Matthew 14:21). It seems that everyone, in their excitement to hear Jesus, forgot to bring any sustenance. At least, no one was willing to admit it, for probable fear they would be trampled on for their food by the masses.

Jesus, seeing the vast multitude and their needs, asked Philip, the disciple from the area:

> "Where are we to buy bread, so that these people may eat?" He said this to test him, for he himself knew what he would do. Philip answered him, "Two hundred denarii worth of bread would not be enough for each of them to get a little" (John 6:5–7).

This question was a faith-check for Philip's level of belief in Jesus. Philip, who had witnessed a multitude of miracles from Jesus, responded with unbelief and self-sufficiency, stating that eight months' wages wouldn't even begin to feed half of them.[1]

Andrew, Simon Peter's brother, gets the tug from a little guy who has bravely come forward to offer his lunch, the biblical equivalent of a Happy Meal of five loaves of barley bread (the coarsest and cheapest grain) and two fish, to Jesus.

> He selflessly gave all he had and trusted Jesus with the outcome, instead of selfishly nourishing his own growling tummy.

I believe Jesus' eyes must have brightened a bit at this little boy's faith, for he knew his Father would always provide. After all, Jesus knew of the crowds' need for food even before they left their homes that morning. And Jesus foresaw this little boy's selfless offering of his entire lunch as a drink offering to his God in the flesh. Then in public reverence to the Father:

> Jesus then took the loaves, and when he had given thanks, he distributed them to those who were seated.

> So also the fish, as much as they wanted. And when they had eaten their fill, he told his disciples, "Gather up the leftover fragments, that nothing may be lost." *So they gathered them up and filled twelve baskets with fragments from the five barley loaves left by those who had eaten.* (John 6:11–13 emphasis mine)

Over fifteen thousand individuals were fed, with plenty of leftovers, all through one single act of obedience. A boy gave all that he had to Jesus. I'm sure that boy looked around and saw all the people eating *his* same barley loaves and fish *he* had so willingly given to his Savior. He experienced firsthand the blessing from his simple act of faith. He selflessly gave all he had and trusted Jesus with the outcome instead of selfishly nourishing his own growling tummy.

God, knowing the pain in our hearts, is asking this same act of sacrifice from us: "Who can you bless? Who have I placed on your heart to pray for, make a meal, fix something for, go shopping for, give a ride to, mow their lawn, visit them, bring flowers to, etc.?" The unforeseen joy that comes from becoming a drink offering during our suffering is like a prickly cactus unexpectedly flowering a vibrant rainbow of blossoms in the arid desert.

We are even commanded by God to joyfully consider our trials: "Count it all *joy*, my brothers, when you meet *trials* of various kinds" (James 1:2 emphasis mine). And during our suffering, we are reminded to:

> *Rejoice in the Lord always*; again I will say, *rejoice*. Let your reasonableness be known to everyone. *The Lord is at hand; do not be anxious about anything*, but in

> everything by *prayer and supplication with thanksgiving* let your requests be made known to God. And the *peace of God, which surpasses all understanding, will guard your hearts and your minds in Christ Jesus.* (Philippians 4:4–7 emphasis mine)

And most importantly, when afflicted, we are to again:

> *Rejoice in our sufferings*, knowing that suffering produces endurance, and endurance produces character, and character produces hope, and *hope does not put us to shame, because God's love has been poured into our hearts through the Holy Spirit who has been given to us.* (Romans 5:3–5 emphasis mine)

"Rejoice and serve others during a trial." I must admit, that's not my first response. Mine is quite the opposite: anger, revenge, sadness, unbelief, and despondency. But this is when a forced act of obedience is essential. Left to our devices, we'd wallow in our misery like pigs in mud. These are the very moments, when there is nothing in the physical world that can provide relief, that we are forced to draw near to God for comfort and experience his deep love for us. As a result, he now becomes our strength (Nehemiah 8:10) as we serve others. Joy is a gift God generously gives his suffering children.

> The unforeseen joy that comes from becoming a drink offering during our suffering is like a prickly cactus unexpectedly flowering a vibrant rainbow of blossoms in the arid desert.

Samuel Rutherford once said, "Whenever I find myself in the cellar of affliction, I always look about for the wine."[2] In the dark basement of deep sorrow, Christians should become steeped in his Word, the Father's source of comfort. The treasures found in Scripture are the only thing that will comfort us. Everything else pales in comparison.

> "Whenever I find myself in the cellar of affliction, I always look about for the wine."
>
> ~SAMUEL RUTHERFORD

Struggling with my seemingly lacking spiritual provision, the Lord again spoke to my heart...

Down to the Dregs

My child, why have you filled your life with meaningless activities to distract you from what you were made to do? You were created for the very purpose to worship me.

Lift your gaze. Focus solely on me. Praise me in advance for your desired outcome. Allow my Spirit to penetrate the dark recesses of your hidden agony, the place where I alone see. I know it is there. That pain is not from me. You live in a fallen world of sin. It is the by-product of your surroundings.

You, through your faith in my Son, are no longer enslaved to your sin, your agony, or your pain. Come to me, those of you who are weary and heavy-laden, and I will give you my rest. My peace I will give you, not as the world gives it. My peace surpasses all understanding. Let not your hearts be troubled. Be not afraid.

I AM in your trial. I AM working all things out for good. I AM your God.

I will never abandon you. *Trust me.*

Place your pain on my altar. Give all of it to me.

I AM big enough to handle it. Allow yourself to be poured out, completely *down to the dregs* for my service. *Do not fear me or your trial.* Watch and see the miracles I perform with your simple act of obedience. The joy you receive will be nothing in comparison to seeing my mighty hand at work. Again, trust me. *I have this too.*

I work all things out for good for those who love me and are called according to my purposes. Just watch and see. I AM still on the throne.

Remember who your God is. Remember who fights for you. Remember whose armor you are wearing. Remember who goes before you and behind you. Remember I AM your God.

Rest in my sovereignty. Allow me to work with your simple acts of obedience. See what I do with your small, seemingly insignificant sacrifice, your Happy Meal.

Watch and see.

For I AM God.

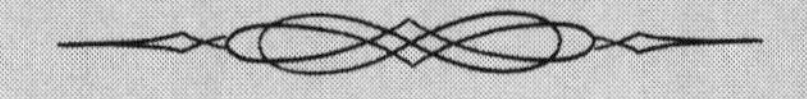

Serving others during our times of suffering is the greatest act of love possible. It's what Jesus did on the cross and what the little boy did with his lunch. It requires submitting to that gentle nudge of the Holy Spirit to bless someone else while we're in pain. It's hard and it requires grace. But that grace and strength to serve others is accessible to us through the cross. That same power that raised Jesus from the dead is available to us through the Holy Spirit (Romans 8:11). For those of you struggling to lift your gaze and serve, this is my prayer for you …

Oh God,

Bless those who are reading this now. Draw close to them.

Help them *lift their gaze* to you, our amazing, on-time, holy, magnificent, and perfect God. Show them that despite their circumstances, you are working all things out for good and your glory. Comfort them.

Breathe your Holy Spirit on them. Fill them. Give them the courage and the faith to become poured-out drink offerings to you. Give them the strength to be drained down to the dregs for your kingdom.

Then fill them up with your Holy Spirit so they are dripping with your love, breathing in your light so that through all the crevasses of their trials, you shine ever more brightly. Turn our people's hearts into a deeper understanding of you and your perfect and complete work on the cross.

You died on the cross for them.

As they walk in obedience and love, give them the strength to serve others when it is difficult to do so. Pour out your joy into them so that people surrounding them would see you and your grace, not their pain during trials.

Use them for your kingdom. Give them confirmation in the flesh that their sufferings are not for naught.

Reveal to them some evidence of grace in their lives, that you have not wasted one tear, one moment of torment, or one time of suffering.

Impart on them your glory. *Bless them.* Increase their faith in you. Give them the boldness to step out in faith in obedience to your perfect leading.

Fill them with your Spirit. Do a mighty work in and through them. Show them how *big* you really are. Remove the scales from their eyes.

Drop the veil from their vision. Allow them to see you with fresh eyes of faith. Fill them with your joy. Use them for your kingdom.

Be glorified, oh God. Be glorified through them.

Shine your Shekinah glory on them. Bless them. Draw so near to them that they are no longer afraid of the pain and agony. Confirm the good fruit and good works you are doing in them in their flesh. Reveal to them what you have already done in their life. Have them lift their gaze and not grow weary.

Keep their focus solely on you, their God, their Savior, and their King.

In Jesus' precious name, I pray.

Amen.

APPLICATION QUESTIONS

Getting to the Heart of It

1. Do you believe it is possible to experience joy during a trial? Why or why not?

2. Have you ever experienced joy while suffering? Describe.

3. Do you believe that all things are possible with God? Why or why not?

4. Have you ever given or served others during a difficult time? Describe.

5. Do you sense that the Lord is asking you to give anything or anyone over completely to him? If so, explain.

6. How does the little boy's act of obedience in faith in giving up his lunch to Jesus while being hungry encourage or discourage you? Why?

> You did not choose me, *but I chose you and appointed you so that you might go and bear fruit*—fruit that will last—and so that whatever you ask in my name the Father will give you. This is my command: *Love each other.*
>
> ~ John 15:16–17 NIV *emphasis mine*

1. Before presenting your prayer requests to God, remind yourself of who God is. List five of God's attributes.

   1 ____________________
   2 ____________________
   3 ____________________
   4 ____________________
   5 ____________________

2. Then list at least five blessings (different ones from previous chapters) in your life that you are grateful for.

   1 ____________________
   2 ____________________
   3 ____________________
   4 ____________________
   5 ____________________

3. Write down your prayer for the faith to serve others in times of difficulty in your life.

4. Write down anything else the Lord is speaking to your heart.

5. Finally, close by praising God to remind yourself of what an awesome God he is. And praise him in advance for whatever the outcome.

SECTION IV

Our Greatest Need

CHAPTER TWELVE

Why Jesus?

And the angel said to those who were standing before him, "Remove the filthy garments from him." And to him he said, "Behold, I have taken your iniquity away from you, and *I will clothe you with pure vestments.*"

~ ZECHARIAH 3:4 *emphasis mine*

Then I heard what seemed to be the voice of a great multitude, like the roar of many waters and like the sound of mighty peals of thunder, crying out, "*Hallelujah! For the Lord our God the Almighty reigns.* Let us rejoice and exult and give him the glory, for the marriage of the Lamb has come, and his Bride has made herself ready; *it was granted her to clothe herself with fine linen, bright and pure*"—*for the fine linen is the righteous deeds of the saints.* And the angel said to me, "Write this: *Blessed are those who are invited to the marriage supper of the Lamb.*"

~ REVELATION 19:6–9 *emphasis mine*

Jesus said to him, "*I am the way, and the truth, and the life. No one comes to the Father except through me.*"

~ JOHN 14:6 *emphasis mine*

I GASPED.

It was beyond glorious.

Right there in front of me during worship, I saw a celestial iridescent light come down from heaven. It gently surrounded the atmosphere of every woman at the conference. The light tenderly yet quickly adhered to each woman, donning her in an amazing white gown.

Each woman's dress was different, unique like herself. Some had intricately placed pearls and others had delicate lace intertwined in the fabric. Each dress completely covered and absorbed the wearer's previously worn garments.

One by one, they looked in amazement at each other's gowns—the workmanship, the breathtaking beauty, and the multifaceted threading. They were dressed from head to toe in the brightest white I had ever seen. The glowing fabric sparkled with life.

The most extraordinary part was that each dress completely covered all of her sins—not a hem of unbelief, not one thread of fear, not a drop of anger, and no evidence of condemnation was seen. Gone were their stains; all were completely consumed by the gown.

Each woman spun around in joy and wonder at her beautiful dress shimmering in the light. The air was filled with laughter and astonishment. Their sins were completely washed away, and they now wore royal white robes.

I was in awe of them.

And then I looked down.

I had one too.

It was so pure. It was spotless. Most importantly, it was holy.

That same radiant light emulated from my vestment as well. The effervescent fabric displayed a kaleidoscope of dazzling pure light with each step. I inhaled its splendor and touched it in disbelief. I had never felt anything that luxurious before.

There were no remnants of the long coat I had worn to church earlier that morning or the thick gray sweater and jeans. I even looked inside the sleeve of my new garment for any trace of the clothes I had put on earlier that morning. There was none. The dress was now one with me; I was wrapped in pure beauty.

The most extraordinary part was that each dress completely covered all of her sins—not a hem of unbelief, not one thread of fear, not a drop of anger, and no evidence of condemnation was seen.

Then, as I looked underneath my arm and down on the floor, I noticed something unexpected. There were no shadows from this vestment. The fabric's own luminosity cast no darkness underneath it. It was its own source of light, created exclusively for and now bound to me.

There we all were, worshiping our Lord and Savior, dressed in our glowing gowns of the finest linens. We looked as if we were ready for our wedding feast with our Savior. We were washed clean, all previous sin eradicated, and clothed in glorious righteousness. We then realized that we were appropriately dressed for the Lamb. It was as if we were finally seeing ourselves as God sees us, washed in splendor.

I exhaled. It was such a beautiful sight to behold, a sea of women, praising the Lord in pure white wedding garments, all because of their faith in Jesus. Without him, we would still be clothed in our sin-stained rags. The righteousness of the Son of God was on each one of us.

For me, that vision was confirmation of the manifestation of the blood of Christ imputed upon us (2 Corinthians 5:21) because of our faith in Jesus. Our Lord even declared it: "'I am the way, and the truth, and the life. No one comes to the Father except through me'" (John 14:6).

> "I am the way, and the truth, and the life. No one comes to the Father except through me."
>
> ~ Jesus Christ

That's why we need Jesus. He's the only way to God.

All paths do *not* lead to God. Jesus is the only way. He is the narrow gate only available to those who declare him as their Savior, "'for the gate is wide and the way is easy that leads to destruction, and those who enter by it are many'" (Matthew 7:13).

We can't depend on our own righteousness to get to God. All our good works, all our attempts to prove ourselves "good enough" to gain access to God, are like disgusting, smelly old rags:

> We have all become like one who is unclean, and all our righteous deeds are like a polluted garment. We all fade like a leaf, and our iniquities, like the wind, take us away. (Isaiah 64:6)

I remember struggling with trying to be "good enough" to get to God. As I confessed my shortcomings to God, I heard, "Do you want to depend on your feeble attempts at righteousness to access a holy God, or the complete work of Christ on the cross that is imputed on all believers?" Head low, I claimed the blood and righteousness of Christ.

We all are helpless and floundering in our sin, our flaws, and our shortcomings. We cannot, nor will we ever be able to, access a holy and perfect God by our good deeds. We need a mediator. And mercifully, God in his infinite love supplied one for us: his one and only Son, Jesus Christ. The apostle Paul affirms:

> For there is one God, and there is one mediator between God and men, the man Christ Jesus, who gave himself as a ransom for all, which is the testimony given at the proper time. (1 Timothy 2:5–6)

"Do you want to depend on your feeble attempts at righteousness to access a holy God, or the complete work of Christ on the cross that is imputed on all believers?"

~ God

We all need Jesus Christ for salvation and for access to our much-needed daily grace from God. As Christians, Jesus is our everything. He is our:

- Alpha and Omega (Revelation 22:13)
- Author and Perfecter of our Faith (Hebrews 12:2)
- Bread of Life (John 6:35)
- Bridegroom (Matthew 9:15)
- Deliverer (Romans 11:26)
- Good Shepherd (John 10:11–14)
- Great I AM (John 8:58)
- Immanuel, God with Us (Matthew 1:23)
- Lamb of God (John 1:29)
- Light of the World (John 8:12)
- Mediator (1 Timothy 2:5)
- Rock (1 Corinthians 10:4)
- Resurrection and Life (John 11:25)
- Truth (John 14:6)
- Word of God (John 1:14)[1]
- Son of God (Matthew 11:27)
- Equal to God (John 5:18)

- Beloved Son (Matthew 12:6)
- Sent by God (Galatians 4:4)
- High Priest (Hebrews 5:5)[2]

Jesus Christ is all those things and so much more. By living a life without sin and then dying in our place on the cross, he paid our debt and reconciled us with a holy God. He's the answer to our greatest need—salvation.

Before I first encountered Jesus, I wondered, *Why do we even need a Savior? Isn't God love? Doesn't he automatically forgive us? And am I really that bad? Doesn't God want us to be with him in heaven?* I must admit when I first accepted Jesus Christ as my Savior, I was unprepared for the revelation of the depth of my sin. Previously, I arrogantly thought of myself as a pretty good person. I compared myself to others and thought, *I haven't killed anyone. I have never cheated on my spouse. I pray daily. I try to show kindness and always give abundantly, so I get a free pass to heaven, right God?*

I felt confused as I attempted to reconcile my depraved state with my desperate need to access a holy God. I realized then that I needed a mediator. I finally understood that apart from Jesus, no one is "good enough" to get into heaven on their own merits, because there is not one righteous, not even one (Romans 3:10).

As I wrestled with these questions, one of my friends suggested reading the entire Bible. I inhaled each word. I was amazed! I thought it would be full of condemnation and would be one long run-on sentence of "Thou shalt not ... " I anticipated it would belabor outdated references that would have no application in today's world.

Here were stories of deceit, bondage, slavery, adultery, murder, and suffering. The interpersonal relations were more intense than some of the cable TV programming I used to watch. I also had a deep conviction that what I was reading was the truth. The contextual analysis of the Bible matched other historical documents I had studied. I had no doubt that these words were true.

The more I read, the more I realized nothing had changed. There was nothing new under the sun (Ecclesiastes 1:9), human beings were still wrought with sin (Romans 3:10), and the wages of sin is death (Romans 6:23). If that was the case, I was in trouble! But apparently, I needed something more.

For me, it took a Christophony, a vision of Jesus Christ, in my living room to transform my life. I was embroiled in a situation I couldn't change on my own. The more I interfered, the worse things got. I was scared. I prayed to God for help and he answered me. He gave me his Son, Jesus Christ, which was all I really needed.

Jesus is our greatest need in our trial. Even though he might not lift the storm, he gives us grace to endure it. That's why we need him. For me, I didn't realize how much I did until he appeared...

Why Jesus?

The vision was so clear, so real, that it terrified me. There was Jesus, right in my living room, in all his holiness, glory, and splendor.

His purity eclipsed the entire room. I didn't even realize I had fallen to my knees. I had *never* seen anything that magnificent before.

I had traveled the world and had seen the most amazing sights: I had hiked the Grand Canyon; scuba dove in the most elaborate Mexican underwater caverns and prismatic coral reefs; skied the breathtaking Austrian alps; inhaled the French Riviera; dappled in the opulence of Monte Carlo; fallen in love with the people of the pearl of Africa, Uganda; trekked through the giant Redwoods; climbed the breathtaking Table Mountain in Cape Town, South Africa; sailed through the Greek Isles; listened to the most beautiful music in Vienna; crossed the Bosporus River in Istanbul; rode in a gondola in Venice; and ate the most extravagant food in France and Italy; but nothing left me wanting like this.

I was undone.

There are no words to describe the splendor that stood before me. Even the intricately chiseled marble statues of Jesus by Leonardo Di Vinci didn't do him justice. I wondered then if Leonardo didn't see Jesus Christ in the flesh when he painstakingly carved those marble blocks, for although those statues look frighteningly realistic, they are bereft of holiness. Nothing on this planet could even come close to the unadulterated beauty I witnessed on that day. Those statues, even though they looked like they could breathe, were like formless shadows compared to what I saw in my living room. The Jesus that appeared to me was real.

Every cell on his body was holy and was in direct opposition to my degeneracy. I was the black velvet cloth the jeweler uses to contrast the brilliance and purity of a flawless diamond. Now I saw that what I perceived as "good" in me was dirty rags compared to his holiness. Then I realized that every cell of my body reeked sin, each one desperately crying out for a Savior.

I was sin. And he was not.

He emanated transcendence. His purity was above that of the world's, for he met the highest standard—God's. This was God in the flesh, the Word who became man.

And there he was in my living room as I cried out to God on my knees.

He was holding out his arms to me. I saw the deep holes in his hands.

He was donned in a simple white glowing gown, and he beckoned me to come to him.

His robes did nothing to obstruct his holiness—it projected right through it.

He had these amazingly piercing eyes, full of pain from my sin, yet still compassionate and deeply caring for the redemption of my soul.

For the first time in my life, I *saw* and *felt* the great price my sin had cost. I finally understood the great penalty he had paid for me—death on that gruesome cross. I finally understood that he died in place of me, so I could approach a holy and perfect God with complete confidence that all my sins were forgiven.

This was the answer to the question I had been searching for all my life; I needed a Savior. I didn't even know what I was looking for; I didn't know I needed one until now. Then I heard it.

The voice was deafening; it physically hurt my ears.

My entire body shook with the booming sound. "*Do you accept my Son as your Savior*?"

My eyes were fixated on those deep liquid golden-brown pools of love from my Savior's eyes—the eyes of sorrow, grieving from sin.

I felt like I had been punched in the stomach; my breath escaped me.

"Yes," was all I was able to croak out of my collapsed windpipe, "Yes, I do."

As quickly as it came, the vision was gone.

The gauntlet was dropped.

I knew with a profound sense of permanency that my life would never be the same again. Although I didn't comprehend it at the time, I was saved from the wrath of God. Jesus was my Savior. I saw the Jesus who died for me.

I finally understood that he received all the punishment for my sins and I was saved from God's wrath and the ravages of hell. I was reconciled with God and would spend eternity in heaven. *And it was all because of Jesus.*

I knew it within every cell in my body, I was a new creation in Jesus Christ.

I was born again.

To Jesus be all the glory!

That vision completely altered my life. I no longer live for myself, but now for Jesus. I'm joyfully his servant. You may never have had a life-changing experience like I did in my living room; that doesn't mean you're not saved. If you have confessed Jesus as your Savior, you are saved. For Jesus even declared it: "'Blessed are those who have not seen and yet have believed (John 20:29).'" Oswald Chambers agrees:

> Being saved and seeing Jesus are not the same thing. Many people who have never seen Jesus have received and share in God's grace. But once you have seen Him, you can never be the same. Other things will not have the appeal they did before.... Jesus appears to those for whom He has done something, but we cannot order or predict when He will come.[3]

Even though we all don't encounter Jesus like I did, we all still need him. It's one of our greatest needs. I thought I was "good enough" until I met Jesus. Now I understand there is nothing that is "good" in me. I agree with Paul when he exclaims, "Wretched man that I am! Who will deliver me from this body of death? (Romans 7:24)." For it seems those who grasp the depth of our depravity, have only done so because they have fathomed the holiness of God, seen or unseen.

Gratefully, my need for a Savior to save me from God's wrath has been fulfilled. I am justified. I am a child of God. I am covered by the blood of Jesus. There are some of you reading this who have trusted in Jesus as your personal Savior.

For it seems those who grasp the depth of our depravity, have only done so because they have fathomed the holiness of God, seen or unseen.

There are others who have not yet taken that step. Either way, allow me to encourage you to lift your gaze. Behold Jesus' majesty, inhale his holiness, and absorb his pureness. See your Savior, the one who provides you access to your God. Confess that you are a sinner and need Jesus to save you from your sins. We have a merciful, forgiving God who desires sweet communion with you. Declare and confirm Jesus Christ as your personal Savior.

Dear God,

Draw near to those who are reading this now. Bless them. Keep them.

Speak to them through your Word, your Holy Bible. Make your face shine down upon them. Help them focus on you, not their pain. May your Word be the only source of comfort in their life. Pour your Holy Spirit into them, fill their greatest need of a Savior.

Bless them, their family, and their health. Give them joy through your Spirit in their times of suffering. Draw near to them, comfort them. Have them realize their desperate need for you in all that they do. Give them your joy, despite their circumstances.

Give them confirmation in the flesh that you're working all things for good and your glory. Do an amazing work in them, through them, and by them. Use them mightily for your kingdom. Ignite in them your fire. Fan the flames of your gifts in them.

Reveal a deeper understanding of you to them.

Call them your friend.

Give them the confidence that through their faith in Jesus, they can boldly approach your throne of grace.

Bless them above and beyond their needs. Show your miraculous hand at work. Use them for your kingdom in ways they thought they could never be a blessing to others. Have them lift their gaze to you, despite their deep waters.

Bless them with your joy and peace that surpasses all understanding.

In Jesus' precious name, I pray.

Amen.

APPLICATION QUESTIONS

Getting to the Heart of It

1. Have you trusted in Jesus Christ as your personal Savior? Why or why not?

2. If yes, write down your testimony.

3. Where do you find the most peace in your times of suffering? Why?

4. What's the most effective prayer you ever prayed?

5. Has there been an action or actions that have completely changed the trajectory of your life? Describe.

6. Do you trust in Jesus to protect you, keep you, provide for you, and bless you even though it means going through trials? Why or why not?

But when you ask, *you must believe and not doubt*, because the one who doubts is like a wave of the sea, blown and tossed by the wind.

~ James 1:6 NIV *emphasis mine*

1. Before presenting your prayer requests to God, remind yourself of who God is. List five new attributes of God.

   1 ______________________________
   2 ______________________________
   3 ______________________________
   4 ______________________________
   5 ______________________________

2. Then list at least five blessings (different ones from previous chapters) in your life that you are grateful for.

   1 ______________________________
   2 ______________________________
   3 ______________________________
   4 ______________________________
   5 ______________________________

3. Write down your prayer for you and your loved ones to look to the cross during times of suffering.

4. Write down anything else the Lord is speaking to your heart.

5. Finally, close by praising God to remind yourself of what an awesome God he is. And praise him in advance for whatever the outcome.

CHAPTER THIRTEEN

The Cross

I lift up my eyes to the hills. From where does my help come? *My help comes from the* L*ORD*, *who made heaven and earth.*

~ PSALM 121:1–2 *emphasis mine*

If the *Spirit of him who raised Jesus from the dead dwells in you*, he who raised Christ Jesus from the dead will also give life to your mortal bodies through his Spirit who dwells in you.

~ ROMANS 8:11 *emphasis mine*

But he said to me, *"My grace is sufficient for you, for my power is made perfect in weakness."* Therefore, I will boast all the more gladly of my weaknesses, so that the power of Christ may rest upon me.

~ 2 CORINTHIANS 12:9 *emphasis mine*

And Jesus said, *"Father, forgive them, for they know not what they do."*

~ LUKE 23:34

For the word of the cross is folly to those who are perishing, *but to us who are being saved it is the power of God.*

~ 1 CORINTHIANS 1:18

Choking, I gasped for breath. My lungs were filled with fluid. Lying in bed was making it worse, and sitting up wasn't helping much.

I looked outside and groaned. It was dark. My phone said 7:12 p.m. Still exhausted, I realized I had slept the whole day. When I'd crawled in bed after my spinning class that morning for "just a little rest," my husband looked at me with his eyebrows raised. I never slept during the day, I exercised five days a week, took daily vitamins and supplements, and ate healthy. I rarely got sick.

Groggy and uncontrollably coughing up mucus, I texted my husband downstairs: *Something is wrong. I can't breathe. I need to go to the urgent care clinic.*

Immediately he came upstairs to our bedroom. "Are you okay?" he asked, sounding worried. "You don't look good."

"I'm not. I can't breathe," I said with a raspy voice while dragging my aching body out of bed. "I don't think I'll make it through the night. We need to go now."

"What? I thought you were just tired. Now you can't breathe?" The anxiousness in his voice increased with each syllable.

I just nodded as I slowly put on my jacket.

I was a shaking, huddled ball in the front seat as we drove to the clinic on the bitter-cold February night. Our concerned five-year-old in the back seat kept repeating, "God, please heal Mommy. Are you okay yet, Mommy?"

I whispered, "Not yet, sweetie. Keep praying."

Gratefully, we were the only ones in the waiting room and I was seen quickly.

The nurse who took my vitals was amazed when I told her how quickly this set in. "Wow. Normally it takes days to get to this point. And you were just a little tired this morning?"

I nodded and tried to stay conscious in between my hacking on the examining table.

The doctor came in. After looking and poking me everywhere, she declared, "You have acute bronchitis and a severe sinus infection. And this just started today?"

"Yes, I was just worn out this morning and slept all day, which is very unlike me," I wheezed out.

"Okay, stop talking. I called in an inhaler, cough medicine, and an antibiotic to your pharmacy. You also have a fever. Here's some extra-strength Tylenol and some Gatorade. Those are all the samples I have left."

Nodding and with trembling hands, I shuddered as I tried to take the pills. The meds weren't going down easy; my throat was almost swollen shut.

She looked at me with concerned eyes as she handed me my release orders. Sounding like a drill sergeant, she said, "Plenty of bed rest, fluids, acetaminophen or ibuprofen every four hours, and take your meds as directed."

I forced a weak smile. "Can you believe I just ran a marathon three weeks ago?"

"No. You look awful. Go home and get some rest."

Miraculously, the prescriptions and inhaler allowed me to sleep throughout the night. I didn't get out of bed for two full days. In between watching every Christian chick-flick on Netflix, I laid in bed snoring like a grizzly bear. My husband came up periodically to make sure I was still breathing.

When I was awake, I prayed to redeem my horizontal time. Faithfully, God spoke to my heart and comforted me as my body healed. He reminded me that sometimes things get worse before they get better, just like they did for his Son, Jesus, right before he went to the cross.

Before I drifted off to sleep, I remembered the night before Jesus was captured and forced to be the defendant at several mock trials. He was in the garden of Gethsemane praying, and knew this hour was upon him. He was sweating droplets of blood (Luke 22:44) and his soul was "overwhelmed with sorrow to the point of death" (Matt 26:38 NIV). Jesus foreknew he was going to be tortured and crucified, yet he still begged his Father to take this cup from him (Luke 22:42). But God didn't answer his Son's prayers as Jesus petitioned—just as God doesn't always give us what we want.

Instead, for Jesus things got much worse. God poured out the totality of his wrath upon his Son on that cross, which resulted in a consecrated holiness swap for all humanity. Through divine intervention and mercy, Jesus absorbed the punishment for our sins. Then Jesus' righteousness was imputed on us—not a fair exchange by any standards. And if God didn't spare his own Son from the cross for our greatest need, then how much more freely will he give us all things (Romans 8:32)?

> And if God didn't spare his own Son from the cross for our greatest need, then how much more freely will he give us all things?

Sometimes God doesn't deliver us from our trials, just like he didn't deliver his own Son from the cross—those times, God delivers us *through* our trials. I can't even imagine what it was like to look up and see God in the flesh, the only sinless man to walk on the earth, being tortured on that cross. He was the spotless innocent Lamb of all humanity, yet there he was nailed to a cross, hemorrhaging blood from every orifice, thorns piercing his head, and struggling for breath. He died an excruciating slow and painful death. And "he was despised and rejected by mankind, a man of suffering, and familiar with pain" (Isaiah 53:3 NIV).

I imagine those same thoughts go through our mind as we look upon the suffering in our lives. Like Jesus' followers, we look up at our cross—our current trial, pain, or suffering—and do not see anything good come from it. We sink into despair, questioning God. And like Jesus' disciples, we might think God blinked and missed this one. We believe that a good God would never let us or his one and only Son suffer in such a horrific manner.

But the cross, through God's amazing grace, alters the trajectory for all eternity for every person ever born. It's where Jesus Christ died for our sins. It's where we need to go during our suffering. It is the only place for true comfort. The cross is a place where we are reconciled with God and where all our debts have been paid. It's where the power of sin is broken in our lives. And it's where we are cured—for by "his stripes we are healed" (Isaiah 53:3 KJV).

Sometimes God doesn't deliver us from our trials, just like he didn't deliver his own Son from the cross—those times, God delivers us *through* our trials.

And it's the only place that makes sense—it's the place of victory. This is where Jesus triumphed over Satan's paltry win with the first Adam. And it's the place for our triumph. It moves our attention and efforts from our current suffering to eternal glory:

> For momentary, light affliction is producing for us an eternal weight of glory far beyond all comparison,

> *while we look not at the things which are seen, but at the things which are not seen*; for the things which are seen are temporal, but the things which are not seen are eternal. (2 Corinthians 4:17–18 NASB emphasis mine)

The cross, and therefore the gospel, is eternal. It is the irrefutable evidence that God cares, sees, and has provided a solution to our pain. Human history climaxes here. It is the defining point for all of us. Without it, we are rejected; with it, we are forgiven. This is the place where mercy, grace, and forgiveness meet.

It's where we go for strength, grace, forgiveness, and rejuvenation. The cross, the very instrument of Roman execution[1], is the ultimate destination for all of us. Either we accept the work done for us on it and spend eternity in heaven, or we reject it for unending, inexplicable, and agonizing torture in hell. For those of us who *receive* the cross, the affliction we experience on earth is the closest to eternal suffering we will ever experience. For those who *do not accept* the cross, the agony on this side of eternity pales in comparison of what is to come in an unending loop of torment.

The cross of Jesus Christ is our greatest need in trials. It is where we cry out to him in complete abandonment and desperation. We grab on to it with every fiber in our being. We cling to the hope and promise that God will never reject us no matter how dark our storm. He is our sustenance; he is the very air we breathe. His Word is the fuel for our starved body and life-giving water to our parched souls. He is everything, and his cross is the only thing we need during our trials.

Our focus needs to be directly on God and his character. Our thoughts must be on his attributes. Our gaze is to be fixated on God's omnipotence. It is essential that we cleave to the knowledge of his omniscience. He is our Savior, our Redeemer, our Covering, our Comforter, and our Great Physician. He is our God.

The old rugged cross is also where we receive access to true divine mercy. It is where we are humbled by the mountain of our own sins so that we can quickly forgive the trivial sins others have committed against us.

The cross of Jesus Christ is our greatest need in trials.

It is where we readjust our focus during our most difficult hours. On this side of the cross, we see the amazing work Jesus has done for us. Instead of feelings of repugnance and horror at this instrument of torture, we experience gratitude and worship to Christ for enduring it for us. It is here that we compare our trials, sufferings, and battles to Christ's, and our self-righteous hearts melt. He received our punishment for our sins on the cross.

> [Jesus] was oppressed, and he was afflicted, yet he opened not his mouth; like a lamb that is led to the slaughter, and like a sheep that before its shearers is silent, so he opened not his mouth. (Isaiah 53:7)

This is where our pain from our current trial is utterly absorbed by the power of the cross. For we deserved the gruesome death that Christ freely suffered. It is here all our pride and pretentiousness dissolve as we lift and affix our gaze on our Savior. It is here we say to God just as Jesus did, "'not my will, but yours, be done'" (Luke 22:42). It is here that we see our desperate need for his grace is readily available. For the same Spirit that raised Christ from the dead lives in us (Romans

8:11). As we cry out to him for strength to weather the storm, he is there. Allow the words from the sons of Korah to comfort you:

> *God is our refuge and strength, a very present help in trouble. Therefore, we will not fear* though the earth gives way, though the mountains be moved into the heart of the sea, though its waters roar and foam, though the mountains tremble at its swelling. There is a river whose streams make glad the city of God, the holy habitation of the most high. *God is in the midst of her; she shall not be moved*; God will help her when morning dawns. The nations rage, the kingdoms totter; he utters his voice, the earth melts. "*Be still, and know that I am God.* I will be exalted among the nations, I will be exalted in the earth!" The LORD of hosts is with us; the God of Jacob is our fortress. (Psalm 46:1–6, 10–11 emphasis mine)

During each step of our trial, we need to make the decision to trust that God is working all things out for good in our lives, despite what it looks like. It is at the cross that faith forges in us "the assurance of things hoped for, the conviction of things not seen" (Hebrews 11:1). It's where our hope and trust in God meet. It's where we begin to blossom into something more extraordinary than we could ever imagine.

This is our final stop—where all our burdens lie. It gives us the grace to look up. We see Jesus' agony for us. He loved us so much that he couldn't let us experience an eternity separated from him. Jesus knew the only way for us to access a holy and perfect God was through a mediator. Who could even begin to attempt to mediate with a holy

God? A mere human? No. All our works are tainted in sin. We all fall short of the perfect, sinless, holy life that God requires.

The only acceptable Mediator would have to be God himself in the flesh, his Son Jesus Christ. According to Jewish tradition, when Jesus stated that God was his father (John 5:18) and called himself the Son of God, he "implied equality with God."[2] Therefore, the only one to mediate on our behalf to a holy God would have to be himself. Jesus was the only one in all creation who could bridge that unfathomable gap on the cross between sinful humans and a holy God.

We realize that our greatest need, a secure eternity with God, has already been met by the perfect work of Jesus Christ on the cross and that our momentary earthly afflictions pale in comparison.

We realize that our greatest need, a secure eternity with God, has already been met by the perfect work of Jesus Christ on the cross and that our momentary earthly afflictions pale in comparison. And so, by our faith in our sinless Savior, we have access to the throne of God:

> For we do not have a high priest who is unable to sympathize with our weaknesses, but one who in every respect has been tempted as we are, yet without sin. *Let us then with confidence draw near to the throne of grace, that we may receive mercy and find grace to help in time of need.* (Hebrews 4:15–16 emphasis mine)

Thankfully, on that cross at Calvary where Jesus died for our sins, God knew exactly what was happening—as did Jesus. Everyone else, like us, was in a complete spiral of disbelief and confusion. Even now as we look at our cross and our larger-than-life trial, we wonder how God could work anything good from it—yet he still does. It just happens in God's perfect timing, not ours.

We, like the disciples, only comprehend the underside of God's amazing eternal tapestry. If we had the eyes of God, we wouldn't change a thing. We would then see the flipside or "right" side of the arras. We would realize the knots of pain, the ball of yarn from a season of suffering and the agony of a lost stitch from a loved one, have created something extraordinary—the most beautifully woven four-dimensional artistical design.

We would grasp that each storm created those majestic spirals of love and flowing streams of forgiveness. We would comprehend that each time we answered someone lovingly instead of lashing out in anger, gleaming crystal water fountains gushing kindness would emerge.

Each time we wrapped our arms and legs around the cross and gently rested our cheek against that worn, tear-stained cross, we would see luxurious trees so tall and massive that they put the Redwoods to shame. We would see those deep caverns from valleys of death are now glorious mountain tops—each one elegantly adorned with blankets of faith and peace that only comes from trusting our Savior.

We would be amazed that each tear we shed is now a glistening jewel intricately laced throughout. When we finally get to see the magnificent awe-inspiring tapestry of our lives, we will praise him for our seasons of suffering. We will praise him for our dark days, and worship him for our painful

Let us then with confidence draw near to the throne of grace, that we may receive mercy and find grace to help in time of need.

~ Hebrews 4:16

moments and natural afflictions. And we will be thankful for the cross because it gave us the strength to endure. When we compare our sufferings to his on the cross, we will finally see how God truly does work all things out for our good and his glory (Romans 8:28 NIV).

The path has already been laid for us. The payment is paid in full. We are forgiven, and through our faith in Jesus Christ we are saved from an eternity in hell. We are now reconciled with God and have the assurance of eternity with him in heaven. Through the cross, we now have access to that divine source of comfort, mercy, grace, and forgiveness, which is what we so desperately need.

I had a vision of the cross. It still haunts me to this day. It transformed my life and view of everyone around me.

The Cross

I saw all the legions of angels in heaven completely astounded and confused.

They were all transfixed on one moment in time, on one person, on a Roman cross. There on that cross, *nailed to that cross*, was God's only Son.

He could have just asked the Father to circumvent this torture as he had all those other times when those foolish people in the synagogue and throughout the city were attempting to stone him. And he could have commanded the legions of thousands of angels to come to his rescue and defend him.

But this is God's only begotten Son? On the cross? And why was there so much blood? *Didn't they know how precious his blood was?*

After all, *blood was life.*

God's only Son's innocent blood was spilling out all over this vulgar instrument of torture that humans used in a frail attempt to enact earthly justice.

There he was, nailed to that cross, in such agony.

Blood bubbled out of his mouth with each labored breath. His swollen, bruised, and beaten body involuntarily convulsed and shook against that cross. His few remaining followers watch in horror and disbelief. Where were all the multitudes that he taught, the ones who had worshiped him as God? Where were the ones he healed? The ones he raised from the dead? And the rest of his followers, where were they? Had they forsaken him too?

He was there, nailed to that cross, completely drenched in his own blood.

Holy, set apart as God's only Son, yet here he was dying on the cross like a worthless, guilty criminal. *And he was innocent!*

Then I saw the most horrible sight; it was worse than seeing him physically suffer with such excruciating pain. I saw the deepest blackness I had ever witnessed.

It was forming into one swarming mass and angrily swirling around in the heavens, picking up speed. It eclipsed the entire sky, the stars, and the universe. It completely overtook everything in its destructive path. And this giant violent whirling magnitude was all being funneled to one point, *all to one person,* dying painfully on the cross, *who was innocent of all sin.*

It was being poured out on Jesus. *It was God's wrath.*

It was as if the physical agony Jesus suffered was nothing compared to the total absorption of all the depravity of humankind and torrential power of God. *All the wrath of God for all sins*—past, present and future—were being spiraled into one point and were piercing into one single being, one innocent Lamb.

It was too much for him, as he gasped with his dying breath, "My God, My God, why have you forsaken me?"

And then after being completely abandoned by his own loving and holy Father, Jesus absorbed *the totality of all of God's wrath for all sinners!*

It was then that Jesus humbly acknowledged his life's mission. He painfully breathed out with the last of his strength and said, *"It is finished."*

He bowed his head and gave up his spirit.

It was finished. The debt for all our sins, shortcomings, mistakes, evil actions, misguiding thoughts, anger, failures, and wicked responses—everything not based in love—was absorbed and paid for in full on that cross on that day.

By our faith in him, we are forgiven. Our sins, once as red as scarlet, are now as white as snow, washed clean by the Savior's blood. We are redeemed. We are reconciled with a holy God. We are saved from wrath. All because of Jesus.

Thank you, Jesus. Thank you for dying in my place on that cross.

Thank you for loving me even until death.
I praise your holy and precious name.

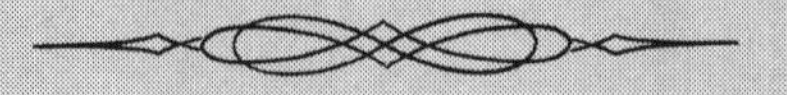

The cross may not be something you have focused on before. Maybe you never grasped the importance of it. Perhaps it never really resonated with you. Possibly, you never fully grasped that someone died in your place. Or you only look to the cross sporadically when you need a reminder of the great price your Savior paid for you.

Whatever camp you are in, this is my prayer for you …

Dear God,

Draw near to my friends reading this. Expand their vision of your Son's perfect work on the cross.

Help them see, feel, and hear what was completed for them on the cross. Break through any strongholds of unbelief that anything they have done or was done to them is too much for your work on the cross. Show them that through the cross, there is no sin that is too big. Speak to their heart, break through any hardness, any lies, and anything that is not of you.

Help them *lift their gaze* to your cross. Help them see that by their faith in your Son as their personal Savior, they are forgiven by a holy God. Help them draw near to the throne of grace available to all who believe in Jesus Christ and confess him as Lord and Savior. Change them from the inside. Change their heart from a heart of stone to a heart of flesh. Pour out your Spirit upon them.

Bless them. Have them call out to you. Comfort them in their affliction. Have them look to the cross and know without a shadow of a doubt they are forgiven, redeemed, and reconciled with a Holy and Perfect God.

Assure them of their place with you in heaven when you call them home. Strengthen them during their temporary journey here on earth.

Help them lift their gaze. Help them realize that this light, momentary affliction is preparing them for an eternal weight of glory beyond all comparison.

Help them look not to the things that are seen but to the things that are unseen, for the things that are seen are transient, but the things that are unseen are eternal. Help them fix their gaze on things that are eternal, on you, on the crown of life that is promised to all who believe in Jesus as their personal Savior.

Give them grace to weather this storm. Give them your peace. Give them your strength. Give them your joy. Bless them, our King.

Do miracles in their life, even if it is just their fixing their gaze on you and not allowing them to wallow in their sufferings. Help them have victory over this battle. Use your cross to humble them. Let them see the great price that was paid for them. And if you had not withheld your only Son from them, give them eyes to see that you will not withhold anything good from them. Show them that the battle has already been won. Fill them with your Spirit. Help them see they are your chosen ones.

They are yours, and like a good Shepherd, you will never let even one go astray. *Draw them in even closer to your sheepfold.*

Surround them with other believers so that they receive just a taste of your love. Fill them again with your Spirit so that they can rise above this trial.

If there is sin in them, reveal it to them and have them repent, turn from it, and leave it at the cross, knowing that all payment was made in full.

Change them into a greater likeness of your Son. Create in them a new being. Bless them. Protect them. Provide for them. Give them your peace. Make your face shine down upon them. Fill them with your Holy Spirit.

In Jesus' precious name I pray.

Amen.

APPLICATION QUESTIONS:

Getting to the Heart of It

1. Describe the role of Jesus Christ in your life as a child and now as an adult.

2. Describe where you go in your time of crisis, trial, or affliction? Do you go to the cross? Why or why not?

3. Describe how you view the cross.

4. Does knowing your greatest need has already been met in a trial comfort you? Why or why not?

5. How does knowing an innocent man died in your place for your sins change your view on life?

6. How can you lift your gaze to Jesus' complete work on the cross when you are experiencing the daily frustrations of life?

"And I will do whatever you ask in my name, so that the Father may be glorified in the Son. *You may ask me for anything in my name, and I will do it.*"

~ JOHN 14:13–14 NIV *emphasis mine*

1. Before presenting your prayer requests to God, remind yourself of who God is. List five of God's attributes (ones you haven't listed yet).

   1 ______________________________
   2 ______________________________
   3 ______________________________
   4 ______________________________
   5 ______________________________

2. List at least five blessings (new ones from previous chapters) in your life that you are grateful for.

   1 ______________________________
   2 ______________________________
   3 ______________________________
   4 ______________________________
   5 ______________________________

3. Write down your prayer to look to the cross during your difficult times.

4. Write down anything else the Lord is speaking to your heart.

5. Finally, praise God to remind yourself that he is an awesome God. Find solace in him.

CHAPTER FOURTEEN

The Throne Room

Why do you pass judgment on your brother? Or you, why do you despise your brother? *For we will all stand before the judgment seat of God*; for it is written, "As I live, says the Lord, every knee shall bow to me, and every tongue shall confess to God." *So then each of us will give an account of himself to God.*

~ ROMANS 14:10–12 *emphasis mine*

SWEAT STUNG MY eyes. Squinting, I looked at my cell phone. It was vibrating off the treadmill shelf.

Not recognizing the number and thinking it was another telemarketer, I rejected the call. Then with arms pumping, I started my simulated uphill sprint.

I kept glancing down at my phone. The voicemail button lit up. During my recovery, I paused my workout praise music and listened to the message.

It was from the school nurse. I stopped running.

The message was garbled. I pushed my bluetooth receiver deeper into my ear. All I could heard was that my son had been in an accident on the bus that morning and I needed to come to school immediately.

Without a second thought, I scooped up all my belongings and walked right off the treadmill. Despite the quick glances and raised eyebrows from the other treadmill-running warriors, I skipped the required disinfectant treadmill wipe-down.

One of my friends called after me, "Where are you going? Aren't you coming to spin class?"

With tears in my eyes, I shook my head and ran to my car. I called my husband, interrupting his business conference. His voice shook and dropped an octave as he agreed to meet me at the school. We quickly prayed on the phone for healing for our son.

I arrived first.

Bursting into the school, I found him. His body looked unusually small and pitiful as he laid on the nurse's couch with an ice pack on his neck. He had dark circles under his eyes. My hands shook and my breathing was shallow—this was every parent's worst nightmare.

Thankfully, he was well enough to be released from school and into our care. We rushed him to the doctor's office and were seen immediately. His injuries were minor, and our son was fine after a few health care visits and some rest.

That one phone call from the school nurse changed our entire day. It could have changed our entire life. Everything stopped. Those catastrophic interruptions happen when we least expect it. I wonder if our predestined appointment with our Creator will be like that phone call I received? Will we be ripped out of our daily routine, like I was that day on the treadmill, to stand before God and account for every action of our life on earth (2 Corinthians 5:10)?

We know it will happen to all of us; there is no escaping it. We just don't know when, and most of us don't think about it often. Our lives are ruled by the tyranny of the urgent. But maybe when God calls us home, it will be a surprise. Or perhaps we'll have some warning. Either way, on that day, our life on this earth will end. We will exit our temporary bodies of flesh. Some of us will have more success; have more money; be more attractive, thinner, healthier; or have more toys than the rest of us. But all of us one day will eventually die.

None of what we thought mattered in this world will matter on the day we face God (Romans 14:12). We will stand in front of him for judgment. For believers, our faith will become sight; for unbelievers, they will cower in fear, now understanding that they have no excuses for sin. They will experience the terrifying fury of God.

> Will we be ripped out of our daily routine, like I was that day on the treadmill, without any warning, to stand before God to account for every action of our life on earth?

In any case, we will all comprehend God's awesomeness. We will be undone by his omnipotence. His omniscience will astound us. Omnipresence will have new meaning. The depth of his magnificence will amaze us. We will finally grasp transcendence and true purity. And eternity will either bring us peace or agony.

In the presence of God's holiness, we will irrevocably comprehend that everything in and about us is tainted in sin. We don't just have a few bad habits; we *are* sin. We will then conclusively discern our necessity to be reconciled with God and our desperate need for a mediator, to even come into God's presence. We will fathom the great mystery of life: that someone must absorb the righteous wrath of God, which is God's just reaction to us, sin in the flesh. We all have this spiritual poverty. Unless we are immersed in Jesus' righteousness and his sinless life is imputed upon us, we will be subjected to God's judgment and spend eternity in unending hell, separated from God. We

> We will fathom the great mystery of life: that someone must absorb the righteous wrath of God, which is God's just reaction to us, sin in the flesh.

will painfully pay for each wicked thought, impure action, white lie, angry word, lustful glimpse, envious glance, and act of retaliation. We will be held responsible for each time we took the Lord's name in vain, didn't honor the Sabbath, disobeyed our parents, and fell short of God's perfect law for our life on earth.

If Jesus absorbed God's punishment for our personal sins on the cross, we are set free. Jesus was very clear on the consequences of our impending judgment:

> "When the Son of Man comes in his glory, and all the angels with him, then he will sit on his glorious throne. Before him will be gathered all the nations, and he will separate people one from another as a shepherd separates the sheep from the goats. And he will place the sheep on his right, but the goats on the left. Then the King will say to those on his right, 'Come, you who are blessed by my Father, inherit the kingdom prepared for you from the foundation of the world.' Then he will say to those on his left, 'Depart from me, you cursed, into the eternal fire prepared for the devil and his angels.' And these will go away into eternal punishment, but the righteous into eternal life." (Matthew 25:31–34, 41, 46)

The stakes of unbelief in Jesus as our personal Savior is beyond huge—it's eternal. It is much bigger than our life here on this earth.

We have a choice: *eternity in heaven with our Creator or in the eternal unquenchable fires of hell.*

Walk gingerly, my friend. Heed the counsel of God incarnate, Jesus Christ. Listen to and obey the gentle tugging at your heart by the Holy Spirit, who urges all of us to reconcile with our Creator. We were created to worship God alone. Without doing what we were created for, we are continually looking for something to fill that God-sized hole in our hearts. The only thing that will fill the emptiness is the Spirit of God through our faith in his Son, Jesus Christ.

We were created to worship God alone.

Lift your gaze, my friend. Your God is there for you. Like a gentleman, his hand is extended to you. He desires an intimate relationship with you. He wants to call you *friend.* God wants you as his child. Accept the free gift of salvation. Don't delay.

Before I leave you and end this book, I want to share one last thing with you. It is my heartfelt desire that your hope is secure. I pray your gaze is lifted to the right place through your trials. I beseech God that your greatest need has been met in your time of suffering. I look forward to your day of judgment when you will be able to declare your faith in Jesus Christ and state, *"I am saved!"*

The Throne Room

I saw the throne room of God. Its beauty was indescribable. The room perfectly reflected the beauty of our Creator, our God. There in the middle on a magnificent golden throne sat our God.

His glory was breathtaking and overshadowed all things.

I couldn't even inhale while standing in the presence of such holiness, pureness, and sinlessness. Even my dependence on air to breathe seemed to be tainted in sin. It was as if my humanity separated me from God. His very existence sucked out all my energy and strength. I realized then that we should need only him. Our lips should only praise God, not curse others, especially our loved ones and enemies.

"Love" was right in front of me. I finally fathomed the depths of "God is love" (1 John 4:8). It just radiated from him.

My eyes now see why humans, as fallen creatures, cannot even enter his throne room or withstand his presence. His awesomeness is too much for a mere mortal.

My throat closed in recompense to his holiness.

I couldn't utter a sound. There he was in all his splendor, the Great I AM.

He reverberated holiness. Everything surrounding him was holy, previously refined, so that no impurities remained. He emitted such an intense energy; I had never experienced anything that powerful before.

I had to put my hands over my ears in fear they might burst. The holy, pure white light that emanated from him burned my eyes. It was too painful to even stand in his presence. The sheer weight of God in all his glory brought me to my knees, then prostrate to the floor in submission. There are no words to describe him. Even if there was, they would melt. My body then responded involuntarily to his holiness and pressed me further down with my face buried into the ground. Reflexive worship was my only response.

"*Holy, Holy, Holy* is the Lord God Almighty," was all that I was even able to formulate in my mind—my mouth could not speak a word. Then I understood Job's revelation, "I had only heard about you before, but now I have seen you with my own eyes" (Job 42:5 NLT).

I now saw and understood what Isaiah proclaimed: "Above him stood the seraphim. Each had six wings: with two he covered his face, and with two he covered his feet, and with two he flew. And one called to another and said: 'Holy, holy, holy is the Lord of hosts; the whole earth is full of his glory! And the foundations of the thresholds shook at the voice of him who called, and the house was filled with smoke.'

And [he] said: 'Woe is me! For I am lost; for I am a man of unclean lips, and I dwell in the midst of a people of unclean lips; for my eyes have seen the King, the LORD of hosts!'" (Isaiah 6:2–5).

As I lay there in his throne room, I was incapacitated. All my works, good deeds, self-righteous acts, all my timeless logs of serving his people and kingdom, faithful prayers, and everything that I thought I would present as an offering, a living sacrifice on my day of judgment to my King on his throne were incinerated—all traces of them were utterly evaporated by his Shekinah glory. I saw how my spiritual pride tainted them. They were all worthless in the presence of such holiness.

All that was left was my faith.

As the dross of my good works burned away, I saw the most beautiful golden-white light in me. It looked like a glowing small seed at first, but it swelled, fueled by his holiness. The light didn't initiate from me; I knew it was from his Holy Spirit—the same Spirit that only comes through faith in Jesus Christ. This light increased until it overtook what was once me. I was so amazed as I looked down at my previous arrogant self of good works and all I saw that was left of me was his Holy Spirit.

I remembered when I first received that seed—it was imparted in me when I first believed Jesus had died for me. It was then I realized I needed a Savior.

Now it was confirmed at such a deeper level of my understanding: I was a sinner and the *only* way I had access to God was because I was covered by the blood of Jesus and his Holy Spirit dwelt in me.

All that remained of me was him in me, through his Spirit by my faith in Christ Jesus. I was therefore saved from the wrath of God.

I would spend eternity with God!

I was saved from the wrath of God!

"*Thank you, Jesus*!" I exclaimed!

With my hands held high, I exhaled a loud, "*Hallelujah*!"

I am reconciled with a holy and perfect God.

I am redeemed!

Now I see how I am declared righteous through Jesus Christ.

And I know that I live by faith (Habakkuk 2:4)!

To God be all the glory!

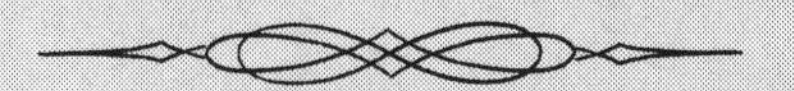

We never know when we will be called into the throne room of God. We all need to be reconciled with God. Before you lay down this book, ask Jesus into your heart if you haven't done so already, *because eternity is a very long time to be wrong.* Release your life to your Savior, Jesus Christ.

To those of you who have already trusted in Jesus as your personal Savior and are now realizing your desperate need for grace, be encouraged. There are no actions, thoughts, or words that will get you any closer to heaven than your faith in Jesus. *It is only by our faith that we are saved.*

Either way, allow the Holy Spirit and the refiner's scalpel to go deeper into your heart. Ask him to search your heart, see if there is anything offensive in you, and lead you in the way everlasting (Psalm 139:23–24). As Christians, we want to walk upright, in opposition to the way of the wicked, the same way the patriarchs of old walked before and after the flood, the way that leads to everlasting life.[1]

It is only by our faith that we are saved.

Submit to what God is gently leading you to do right now through his Spirit. Pray and join me as I cry out to him …

Dear Jesus,

Draw near to my friends who are reading this now. Help them *lift their gaze*. Help them see and understand the complete and final work your Son did on the cross for them. Help them see your Son; because of his infinite love for them, he would go to that cross just for them if he needed to.

To those who have not confessed you, Jesus Christ, as their Savior, have them proclaim the prayer of old:

> Jesus, I need you. I am a sinner. I am not perfect. I need you as my personal Savior. I need to be saved from your wrath. You are the only holy, sinless, all-powerful being, the Great I AM. Come into my heart, Jesus. Change me. Release me from the bondage of my sins. Make me more like you. I need you. Help me, Jesus, to remember my daily need for you. I want to be able to withstand the presence of God in his throne room on my day of judgment. I know I can only do that by your grace, through my *faith in you*. Pour out your Holy Spirit in me. I want to become one of your children. I want to be forgiven. I want to be saved. I want to spend eternity with you.

To those who already know you as their Savior, help them, Jesus, be obedient to the gentle leading of your Holy Spirit. Give them the desire to bless others, to serve others in their times of need. Help them see what others have failed to see and to bless the lacking in someone's life. Help them show Christ to those who need to see you, Jesus, to those who need hope, and your love. Keep them well-grounded and anchored in your Word. Help them to worship you and you alone. Help them not put their trust in anything other than you, their God. Don't let their feelings dictate their past, present, or future.

Help all of us walk in righteousness, in a way that glorifies you. Have us daily ask you to search our hearts, see if there are any grievous ways in us that we are blind. Convict us and remove the bondage of sin from our lives. The same power that raised Jesus from the dead, dwells in us. We are no longer slaves to sin. We are set free!

Use us and our freedom mightily for your kingdom. In whatever situation you plant us in, help us bloom with the fragrant love of Christ, making us a sweet-smelling aroma of love for all, drawing us closer to Jesus.

Help us, Lord, be more like you.

When others see us, have them see you in us.

Help us stand *firm in the truth* of your Word. Give us a greater understanding of your Word. Help us apply it to our lives. Lift our gaze, oh God.

Help us see how *big* you really are, the Great I AM. Assist us in laying down all our burdens on your altar.

Take our worries, wrap your loving arms around us and our loved ones.

Protect us from all harm. Use us to bring glory to your name. And despite what is swirling around us, change each one of us. Give us your joy!

In Jesus' precious name, I pray.

Amen.

APPLICATION QUESTIONS

Getting to the Heart of It

1. What do you think you will say to God when you stand before him on that day of judgment?

2. What are things you wished you didn't do, say, or think? List some of them.

3. How do you think you will be able to justify the actions, words, or thoughts you listed above, to a holy God?

4. Do you believe the punishment for all your sins has been paid for on the cross? Why or why not?

5. Will Jesus Christ be your covering and defense on your day of judgment? Why or why not?

6. Do you believe that *all* your actions are covered and paid for by the cross? Why or why not?

7. List any areas of unforgiveness or bitterness that you haven't given over to God in repentance. Ask someone you trust to pray for you in this area.

8. How can you show gratitude to Jesus for the gift of being able to one day stand in the throne room of God on your day of judgment (for example, walking in a manner worthy, obeying his commands, praying without ceasing, etc.)?

9. How does the knowledge that Jesus met your greatest need—reconciling you and giving you access to a holy God—alter your worship of him?

In my distress I called upon the L*ORD*; to my God I cried for help.
From his temple he heard my voice, and *my cry to him reached his ears.*

~ PSALMS 18:6 *emphasis mine*

1. Before presenting your prayer requests to God, remind yourself of whom you are praying to. List your five favorite, most heartfelt attributes of God.

    1 ______________________________
    2 ______________________________
    3 ______________________________
    4 ______________________________
    5 ______________________________

2. List your top five blessings in your life that you are most grateful for and how these have changed throughout the book.

    1 ______________________________
    2 ______________________________
    3 ______________________________
    4 ______________________________
    5 ______________________________

3. List your prayer requests.

4. Write down anything else the Lord is speaking to your heart.

5. Finally, praise God in advance for whatever the outcome, despite the circumstances in your life.

CHAPTER FIFTEEN

Conclusion

The LORD is my shepherd; I shall not want. He makes me lie down in green pastures. He leads me beside still waters. He restores my soul. He leads me in paths of righteousness for his name's sake. Even though I walk through the valley of the shadow of death, I will fear no evil, for you are with me; your rod and your staff, they comfort me. You prepare a table before me in the presence of my enemies; you anoint my head with oil; my cup overflows. *Surely goodness and mercy shall follow me all the days of my life, and I shall dwell in the house of the LORD forever.*

~ PSALM 23:1–6 *emphasis mine*

S*MACK!*

The ball landed in the soft webbing of my mitt. Effortlessly, I would toss it into my right hand and fire it back.

I experienced the same vision every time I ran: catching a fast-pitched softball and whizzing it back, repeatedly.

Then during one Sunday worship service, it all made sense. I saw the vision again—the ball coming and landing hard in my mitt—but this time, I gently dropped it to the ground. Then I looked up and prayed, "God, can you field these?"

Instantly a large, thick light gray cloud in the shape of an oyster shell formed in front of me. In my mind's eye, I laid down my softball mitt and got down on one knee to pray.

All the balls were enveloped by this huge misty screen. I didn't even see or hear them come at me any longer. I just prayed.

Then I heard him speak: "You, in your own strength, were trying to catch and return all these. They were never meant for you. I am your shield, your banner, your provider, and your protector. This is my responsibility."

Smiling, I nodded. I was never meant to deal with all the enemy throws at me—that's God's job. It's my job to pray and trust God.

As you conclude this book, I pray your heart is lighter, your gaze is lifted, and your view of God's amazing work in you is irrevocably transformed. It is my heart's desire that you have a deeper revelation of how much God loves you and how much he desires a personal relationship with you.

> "You, in your own strength, were trying to catch and return all these. They were never meant for you. I am your shield, your banner, your provider, and your protector. This is my responsibility."
>
> ~ God

I implore you to go to God with your pain, anger, and fear. I pray that your prayer life, your expression of worship, your hunger for God's Word, and your view of your Creator has grown much richer, deeper, and more passionate because of this book.

It is my hope that, despite any suffering you are experiencing, God heals your heart and you have peace. I pray your belief is firm in who is with you in the fire, goes before you in battle, and turns your spiritual Happy Meal into divine nourishment for thousands.

As you put on the whole armor of God each day, it is my heart's desire that your knowledge and understanding of God is bigger than your trials. And finally, that the cross of Jesus Christ is the place where you find comfort, forgiveness, and peace knowing your greatest need—reconciliation with a holy God—has already been met by your Savior Jesus Christ.

I hope this book consoled you as it did me. As I was traversing through my storms, I was grateful that God, despite *all* my initial protests, used me to be his scribe for this book. I was beyond blessed in the process. I am eternally thankful that God draws near us and comforts us in our times of affliction.

I pray this book challenged and changed you as it changed me.

In closing, I pray the priestly blessing over you and your loved ones:

> The LORD *bless you and keep you*;
> the LORD *make his face to shine upon you and be gracious to you*;
> the LORD *lift up his countenance upon you and give you peace.*
> (NUMBERS 6:24–26 *emphasis mine*)

In Jesus' precious name I pray.
Amen.

Acknowledgements

I WOULD NEVER HAVE been able to write this book without my Lord and Savior Jesus Christ. The sweet words of comfort I received in writing and editing this book were my lifeline in my dark days. Thank you, Jesus, out of all the people in the earth, you chose me to share these words.

I am so thankful for my greatest cheerleader in the trenches, my best friend and my hero—my husband. His tireless support, and editing and proofreading skills were invaluable. I couldn't have done it without you undergirding me. I am so grateful for you, my love.

My children were amazing, releasing me to pour my heart, soul, and time into this book. I thank Jesus for each of you.

Thank you, Karen Randall, Ava Pennington, Beth Veenema, Diana Freccia, Tanya Cramer, Christy Distler, and Stephanie Anderson for your incredible editing skills. This book would not have come to fruition without you!

I have been so blessed to sit under the preaching and teaching of the current and previous pastors of Covenant Fellowship Church: Jared Mellinger, Mark Prater, Marty Machowski, Andy Farmer, Rob Flood, Jim Donohue, Joseph Stigora, Doug Hayes, Joel Shorey, Kenny Lynch,

David Sharp, Brian VanderWeide, and Dave Harvey. As well as the pastors at Trinity Community Church: Steve Trader, Robert Kossak, Debbie Keever, Laura Piraino, and Trish Gunn. And the pastors and staff at First Baptist Orlando, especially David Uth, Danny De Armas, Chris Ogden, David Loveless, and Erin Warren.

Wilbroad Chanda, thank you for all your help and the amazing foreword you wrote for this book. I am so grateful for you and Zicky.

My heart swells with appreciation for Marlene Bagnull's Greater Philadelphia Christian Writers Conference and her advanced writers' critique group. Your wise words spurred me to become a better writer.

To Jere Thompson Jr. and Chris Chambless, the founders of Ambit Energy, I am deeply indebted for your efforts, for without them I would never have been afforded the time freedom to complete this work. Ray Montie, Jordan Bank, Darrell Starkweather, and all those at Ambit Energy, thank you for your heroic efforts to help us succeed.

Also, I'm beholden to the staff at The Well Coffeehouse and Marketplace in Hockessin, Delaware, for being such a gracious host to me as I wrote and rewrote many of the pages of this book.

To all the prayer warriors God has so generously placed in my life and the ladies in my previous Bible studies I've attended and led, your love, support, and care have been like manna in the wilderness to me. Thank you for your encouragement and prayers. And to the many people who have painstakingly encouraged and prayed for me, *thank you*!

I am honored to labor alongside all of you.

Most importantly, I want to thank God for my trials. If he hadn't given them to me, I wouldn't have run two marathons, met so many extraordinary people, written this book, and grown daily and exponentially more in Christ.

Thanks again, God. You know best.

To God be all the glory!

Notes

Foretaste: Deep Waters

1. *Merriam-Webster Dictionary, s.v.* "trial," accessed October 13, 2017, http://www.merriam-webster.com/dictionary/trial.

Chapter Two: Why Me?

1. Nathaniel Gronewald, "One-Quarter of the World's Population Lacks Electricity," *Scientific American*, November 24, 2009, accessed September 21, 2017, https://www.scientificamerican.com/article/electricity-gap-developing-countries-energy-wood-charcoal/.
2. "Isaac Newton > Quotes > Quotable Quote," *Goodreads*, accessed October 18, 2017, https://www.goodreads.com/quotes/232390-trials-are-medicines-which-our-gracious-and-wise-physician-prescribes.

3. "Esther—Queen—Bible Woman," *Women in the Bible*, accessed May 16, 2016, http://www.womeninthebible.net/1.14.Esther.htm.
4. "The Jewish Temples: The Babylonian Exile," *The Jewish Virtual Library*, accessed May 16, 2016, http://www.jewishvirtuallibrary.org/jsource/History/Exile.html.
5. "Esther—Queen—Bible Woman," *Women in the Bible*, accessed May 16, 2016, http://www.womeninthebible.net/1.14.Esther.htm.

Chapter Four: Eyes on God

1. *Cambridge Bible for Schools and Colleges Commentary,* Genesis 3, *Bible Hub*, accessed January 19, 2018, http://biblehub.com/commentaries/cambridge/genesis/3.htm.
2. *Keil and Delitzch OT Commentary*, Genesis 3, *Bible Hub*, accessed January 19, 2018, http://biblehub.com/commentaries/kad/genesis/3.htm.
3. "Commentaries, Isaiah 14:12," *Bible Hub*, accessed March 17, 2018, http://biblehub.com/commentaries/isaiah/14-12.htm.

Chapter Five: Do You Trust Me?

1. *Cambridge Bible for Schools and Colleges Commentary,* Job 1, *Bible Hub*, accessed January 19, 2018, http://biblehub.com/commentaries/cambridge/job/1.htm.
2. "Elohim-Jehovah," *Bible Hub*, accessed January 19, 2018, http://biblehub.com/topical/e/elohim-jehovah.htm.

3. *Cambridge Bible for Schools and Colleges Commentary,* Job 1, *Bible Hub,* accessed January 19, 2018, http://biblehub.com/commentaries/cambridge/job/1.htm.
4. Ibid
5. *Sources of the Pentateuch, Bible Hub,* accessed January 19, 2018, http://biblehub.com/library/gladden/who_wrote_the_bible/chapter_iii_sources_of_the.htm.
6. *Barnes Notes on the Bible,* Job 1:3, *Bible Hub,* accessed May 24, 2018, http://biblehub.com/commentaries/job/1-3.htm.

Chapter Six: The Waters Will Not Overtake You

1. *Ellicott's Commentary for English Readers, Bible Hub,* accessed, January 18, 2018, http://biblehub.com/commentaries/ellicott/jonah/1.htm.
2. *Ellicott's Commentary for English Readers, Bible Hub,* accessed January 24, 2018, http://biblehub.com/commentaries/ellicott/jonah/4.htm.
3. "Lake Marion, South Carolina," *SCIWAY,* accessed May 16, 2016, http://www.sciway.net/city/lake-marion-sc.html.

Chapter Seven: I Know Your Pain

1. "Commentaries, Genesis 37:20," *Bible Hub,* accessed January 25, 2018, http://biblehub.com/commentaries/genesis/37-20.htm.

2. *Matthew Henry's Commentary on the Whole Bible*, Romans 4, *Bible Hub*, accessed January 23, 2018, http://biblehub.com/commentaries/mhcw/romans/4.htm.
3. Philip Kosloski, "How much might Judas' 30 pieces of silver be worth today?" *Aleteia*, April 12, 2017, accessed January 23, 2017, https://aleteia.org/2017/04/12/how-much-might-judas-30-pieces-of-silver-be-worth-today/.
4. "Scourging and Crucifixion in Roman Tradition," *Truth of God, Restoring Christianity for Today*, accessed January 23, 2018, https://www.cbcg.org/scourging-crucifixion.html.
5. Ibid.
6. Ibid.

Chapter Eight: Amazing Grace

1. "Amazing Grace | John Newton," published 1779, *Timeless Truth*, accessed May 16, 2016, http://library.timelesstruths.org/music/Amazing_Grace/.
2. "Commentaries, John 11:35," *Bible Hub*, accessed January 25, 2018, http://biblehub.com/commentaries/john/11-35.htm.

Chapter Nine: Know Who Fights for You

1. *MacLaren's Exposition of Holy Scripture*, Exodus 17:15, *Bible Hub*, accessed January 26, 2018, http://biblehub.com/commentaries/exodus/17-15.htm.
2. Ibid.
3. Ibid.

4. Ibid.
5. "Commentaries, Exodus 3:14," *Bible Hub*, accessed January 26, 2018, http://biblehub.com/commentaries/exodus/3-14.htm.

Chapter Ten: The Whole Armor of God

1. "Corrie Ten Boom," *Brainy Quote*, accessed May 16, 2016, http://www.brainyquote.com/quotes/quotes/c/corrietenb393675.html.
2. *Matthew Henry's Concise Commentary*, Ephesians 6, *Bible Hub*, accessed January 30, 2018, http://biblehub.com/commentaries/mhc/ephesians/6.htm.
3. Ibid.
4. Ibid.
5. Ibid.
6. Ibid.
7. Cameron Buttel, "Fresh Snow on Luther's Dunghill—What Evangelicals Forget and Catholics Don't Get," *the bottom line* blog, December 18, 2009, accessed May 10, 2016, http://onceuponacross.blogspot.com/2009/12/fresh-snow-on-luthers-dunghill-what.html.
8. Albert Barnes, *Notes on the Bible* [1834], *Sacred-Texts*, accessed May 10, 2016, http://sacred-texts.com/bib/cmt/barnes/eph006.htm.
9. Ibid.
10. Ibid.

11. *Matthew Henry's Concise Commentary*, Ephesians 6, *Bible Hub*, accessed January 30, 2018, http://biblehub.com/commentaries/mhc/ephesians/6.htm.
12. *Strong's Concordance*, Greek, 3162.machaira, *Bible Hub*, accessed February 7, 2018, http://biblehub.com/greek/3162.htm.
13. Ibid.
14. "Commentaries, Ephesians 6:18," *Bible Hub*, accessed May 4, 2018, http://biblehub.com/commentaries/ephesians/6-18.htm.
15. *Matthew Henry's Concise Commentary*, Ephesians 6, *Bible Hub*, accessed January 30, 2018, http://biblehub.com/commentaries/mhc/ephesians/6.htm.
16. Ibid.
17. Ibid.

Chapter Eleven: Down to the Dregs

1. *Matthew Henry's Commentary*, John 6:1–14, *Bible Gateway*, accessed May 11, 2016, https://www.biblegateway.com/resources/matthew-henry/John.6.1-John.6.14.
2. "Samuel Rutherford Quotes," *Good Reads*, accessed May 14, 2016, https://www.goodreads.com/author/quotes/197580.Samuel_Rutherford.

Chapter Twelve: Why Jesus?

1. "Dictionary of Biblical Themes – 2203 Jesus Christ, titles and names of," *Bible Gateway*, accessed May 15, 2016, https://www.biblegateway.com/resources/dictionary-of-bible-themes/2203-Jesus-Christ-titles-names.
2. "Dictionary of Bible Themes – 2218 Jesus Christ, Son of God," *Bible Gateway*, accessed May 15, 2016 https://www.biblegateway.com/resources/dictionary-of-bible-themes/2218-Jesus-Christ-Son-God.
3. Oswald Chambers, "Have you seen Jesus?" *My Utmost for His Highest*, April 9, accessed March 12, 2018, https://utmost.org/have-you-seen-jesus/.

Chapter Thirteen: The Cross

1. "14 Types of Ancient Christian Crosses," *Orthodox Christianity*, accessed February 11, 2018, http://orthochristian.com/97480.html.
2. "Bible Commentary, John 5:18," *Bible Hub*, accessed February 12, 2018, http://biblehub.com/commentaries/john/5-18.htm.

Chapter Fourteen: The Throne Room

1. *Gill's Exposition*, Introduction to Psalm 129, *Bible Hub*, accessed March 7, 2018, http://biblehub.com/commentaries/gill/psalms/139.htm.

For additional content and resources for leaders, please visit:

www.deepwatersliftyourgaze.com

A portion of the proceeds of this book goes toward providing hope to the incarcerated through Lift Your Gaze, a 501(c)3 organization through Capstone Legacy Foundation.

For more information about Lift Your Gaze's initiatives to reach the darkest areas of our society or to make your tax-deductible donation, go to www.liftyourgaze.org or scan the QR code below.

Thank you for your support.

Lift Your Gaze,
Kim M. Clark
Author, Publisher, & Founder

Made in the USA
Columbia, SC
16 April 2023